Bicycle Repair

by the editors of *Bicycling*® magazine

Rodale Press, Emmaus, Pennsylvania

Senior Editor, Ray Wolf
Edited by Larry McClung
Cover photograph by Mark Lenny
Cover design by Linda Jacopetti and Karen A. Schell
Book design by Linda Jacopetti

Library of Congress Cataloging in Publication Data
Main entry under title:

Bicycle repair.

    Cover title: Bicycling magazine's bicycle repair.
    1. Bicycles—Maintenance and repair.   I. Bicycling!
II. Title: Bicycling magazine's bicycle repair.
TL430.B53   1985   629.28'772   85-1858
ISBN 0-87857-543-X   paperback

   4   6   8   10   9   7   5   3   paperback

Contents

Introduction

Spring is the time when many of us haul our bikes out of a dark corner where they have idled all winter, eager to get them in condition for another riding season.

In some cases, the bikes go straight onto the bike rack for a quick journey to the local bike shop. Soaking a chain in kerosene, cleaning road film off of brake pads, and changing frayed derailleur cables are not the preferred weekend activities of some bike owners.

But others of us eagerly clean off the work bench, set out some tools, and prepare to spend a few pleasant hours tinkering with our bikes. For us, spring bike tune-up is more than just a necessary annual chore. It is a time for reflecting on last season's rides and thinking about ways to improve our bike's performance. It provides an opportunity to check parts for wear and fatigue, to anticipate and thus avoid potential breakdowns during the new riding season, and in general it gives us time with our bikes before the riding season.

There are many good reasons for knowing how to do at least some of your own bicycle repairs. For one thing, springtime brings a backlog of work to most shops. If your bike requires only a light tune-up, you can do the job at home and be off and riding while your friends are still waiting to get their bikes out of the shop.

An even better reason to do your own repairs is that it helps you become familiar with your bike. In the course of a general tune-up, you will look at and listen to all parts of your bike more closely than you would were you to cart the bike off to a shop. Such close scrutiny may reveal the need for preventive maintenance or repairs. Such attention will help to prevent breakdowns later in the season during an enjoyable ride in the country, far from any repair shops. Plus, time spent repairing your bike will better prepare you to cope with any problems that do arise when you are on the road.

So if you've never worked on your bike before but are tempted to try, we say, "Go ahead and do it!" But you say, "I'm no mechanic; how do I begin?"

There are lots of different ways to learn. The time-honored initiation comes in childhood. Something on your old clunker breaks, and you pick up a pair of pliers and a hammer. You either fix the bike or you nearly destroy it. From such humble beginnings are master mechanics made.

For those not quite as brave, your best bet may be to attend a class in basic bike mechanics. These are often available in night school programs. They are also often sponsored by local hardware stores, bicycle shops, and bike clubs.

Bike clubs are usually an excellent source of mechanical expertise. Whether you have no mechanical skill whatsoever or are a certified rocket engineer who simply has never worked on a bicycle, your local club may be the best place to learn what's what. You may find that classes are a regular club activity. Failing that, you can probably locate a member who is mechanically inclined and who would be glad to help you learn more about your bike's inner workings.

Having a tutor is undoubtedly the best way to learn mechanical skills. You benefit from your teacher's experience, the use of his or her tools while you're learning, and you don't have to search for days for answers to simple questions—you just ask. But you can also learn from books, such as the one you are now holding in your hands.

Bicycle repairs are, for the most part, quite simple and easy to learn. The first time around you may be a little unsure whether you put your bearings back into your headset correctly or whether your bottom bracket is too loose or too tight. But after doing a particular job once or twice, your confidence will grow, and you will wonder why you waited so long to give it a try.

If you already have some basic mechanical skill, the written advice gathered together in this book should suffice to get you off to a confident start. And if you can find a knowledgeable friend to check your work in the earlier stages, so much the better.

While the ideas and instructions offered on the following pages represent the cumulative wisdom of many experienced cyclists, problems may arise that we have not addressed in a way that seems to work for you. If so, don't hesitate to check other repair manuals. The more slants you can find on a particular repair job, the better your chances of understanding it. And while you are comparing sources, don't overlook the repair manual that came with your bike.

The Editors,
Bicycling magazine

Part One
Preparing to Make Repairs

Basic Tools and Skills

Before you can seriously start working on your bike, you need to assemble a basic collection of tools. One way to do this is to go to a bike shop or hardware store and buy every tool you think you'll need or the salesperson recommends. Although this course of action gets you working quickly, it has some rather obvious drawbacks.

There is a slightly modified version of this plan, that advises buying a basic "universal" bike tool kit as a starting point, but we think this is less than ideal. You'll end up with stuff you'll never use.

A better method is to buy each tool as you need it for each job you tackle. In this way, you'll spread out the expense, and since you're buying a specific tool for a specific job for a specific bicycle, you'll end up with a custom tool kit that fits your bike precisely. Ill-fitting "universal tools" are the bane of a good mechanic's life.

When you buy tools, don't skimp on quality, unless you're planning to use the tool only once. If it's a tool you'll use again and again, buy the best you can afford. Good tools repay your investment by not rounding off nuts and bolts, by not breaking, by not suddenly giving way and skinning your knuckles, by not slipping and scratching your bike's beautiful paint job, and by not being so clumsy that they're useless for half the jobs they're supposed to accomplish. In general, bike shops are the best place to buy special bike tools, while hardware stores are better for sockets and wrenches.

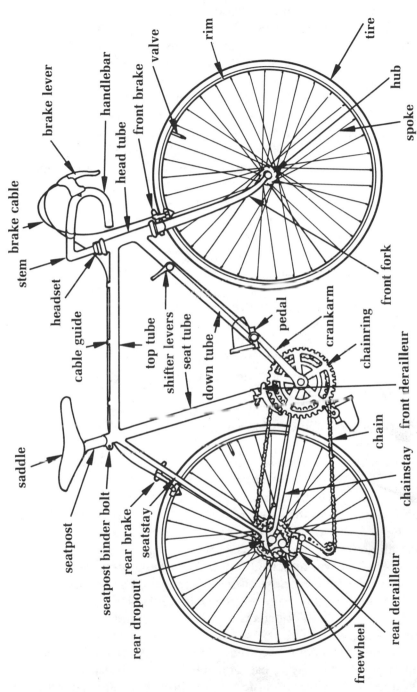

Illustration 1–1. The anatomy of a bicycle.

Which tools you purchase depends in part on the context in which you expect to use them. When repairs are made at home, the size and weight of the tools used are less important than their ability to perform the work well. By contrast, size and weight are major considerations when selecting tools to carry on your bike for on-the-road repairs. Eventually, you will find yourself wanting two tool kits. The one reserved for home use will contain specialized bike tools that are chosen for their uniqueness and dependability. The one assembled for mounting on your bike will contain tools chosen for their lightness and their ability to perform more than one task.

Although you will have different tools for different types of repair, the basic mechanical skills needed to repair a bike are the same, regardless of where you are working on your bike. These skills are hard to describe in detail, but the usual litany consists of principles and rules such as the following:

- Always clean parts before assembling them.
- Always lubricate parts that fit together.
- Never use force.
- Always use the right tool for the job.
- Never improvise a tool unless you know what you're doing. Then think twice about using it.
- Never use a hammer or heat except when repair instructions specifically call for one or the other.

Take your time. Rushing a job usually ruins it.

To develop that elusive "mechanic's feel," remember that most bicycle parts are comparatively fragile. Thus, it's better to undertighten them than to screw them down until they shriek. To check your work, go around the bike after a ride and check the tightness of the various fasteners. If some are loose, then you know that you undertightened them. Snug them down and check them again the next time. In this way, you'll learn how tight is tight, without the expense of replacing lots of little stripped aluminum doodads too frail to withstand your brutish treatment.

The only exception to this rule is with brake parts, which should be as tight as you can get them without breaking them. If you do strip a brake cable anchor bolt, be grateful for the knowledge you've gained. Most good mechanics learned how to tighten those bolts in exactly the same way. The consequences implicit in a loose brake part are too awful to justify a light hand in this case.

Before you pick up your first wrench, be prepared to make a mistake or two. Bicycle repair generally is fairly straightforward. The way you fix something on one bike is basically the way you fix it on a different brand. There are a few minor differences, but the technique remains the same. However, bicycle parts often differ greatly from one brand to another. You will learn over time to pay special attention to what brand of replacement part you are getting. Get to know the person you will be dealing with to buy parts. Make sure you know the brand names and model numbers of your major components before you go out to buy your parts.

Finally, remember that fixing your bike should be fun; it really should be. It's satisfying, rewarding, and provides you with lots of skills that carry over into other jobs. You may not want to exercise these, however, or even let anyone else know you possess them. If word of your newfound mechanical expertise becomes public, you may be besieged with pleas for fix-it help from every quarter. In this case, the bicyclist's strategy is obvious—put down your tools and go for a ride.

A Custom Tool Kit for the Road

One of the delights of bicycling is that you can get away from civilization. Even while staying on paved roads, you often find yourself miles from the nearest phone.

Is this an advantage or a disadvantage? If you are self-sufficient on your bike, it's clearly an advantage. But if you can't make simple repairs or steer clear of simple breakdowns, you may find the freedom of bicycling more threatening than refreshing.

The best way to learn simple repairs is to practice before you leave the protective safety of home. Read all the chapters in this book carefully, acquire a good set of tools, and set aside an afternoon to explore your bike's working parts. It's time well spent.

As your confidence in yourself, your bike, and your repair skills grows, you'll find yourself taking longer rides. On long rides, you'll want to carry the tools and spare parts you need to disassemble and overhaul the working mechanisms of your bike. Since the exact tools required vary from bike to bike, a prepackaged tool kit will probably include tools you don't need and not include tools you do need. It's far better to know what your bike's requirements are and assemble your own tool kit.

Even though you'll be customizing your tool kit, there are some things you'll want to have for sure. The list below should serve as a starting point. As you work on your bike, you'll develop a feel for what might need repair and what you know you've already taken care of.

Stamped steel wrenches with tire irons for handles are very useful. These palm-size wrenches don't stand up to shop use, and they look crude, but they are adequate for on-the-road repairs, and they save lots of weight and space. You compensate for the tools' crude nature by working more slowly and carefully. The tire irons work very well. A six-inch, adjustable wrench works where the stamped steel wrenches don't and vice versa.

A pocketknife, armed with plenty of strangely shaped blades, has all sorts of uses you might not anticipate. For example, the file/hacksaw blade can be used for various emergency repairs, the woodsaw for campfires, and the tweezers for handling ball bearings.

You should carry something to cut control cables—the best answer is to carry a pair of needle-nose pliers with a built-in wire cutter; these pliers serve double duty when you need to clamp a brake or derailleur cable.

You still aren't finished with pliers, though. Sometimes you need pliers with shorter, wider jaws than needle-nose pliers. Buy a pair of pocket-size arc-joint pliers, such as those made by Channellock. These pliers offer a wide range of jaw spacings that fit all sorts of parts. Moreover, they can be used as headset tools. Buy a pair that will enable you to tighten or loosen a standard 32-millimeter headset locknut, allowing for instant on-the-road repair.

The most common touring malfunctions are broken spokes and flat tires. For flat tires, your repair kit is obvious—spare tubes, patch kit, and for longer tours, a spare tire. For broken spokes, you need a spoke wrench (they come in different sizes; make sure yours fits your spoke nipples) and a way of getting your freewheel cogs (or sprockets) out of the way. Of course, you also need the correct size replacement spokes.

To remove a whole freewheel you will need a special freewheel remover and a big tool to grab the freewheel remover and turn it—either a bench vise or a big (12-inch) adjustable wrench. Since it's usually difficult to find someone with a special freewheel remover, buy one and count on borrowing a large wrench or vise. (When you're touring far away from farms, homes, and gas stations, a greater percentage of motorists you meet will be driving pickup trucks with well-stocked tool boxes.)

Another problem you may run into is rim damage. For this problem, there is no substitute for your own mechanical skill. When a pothole gets you, you may have to use a rock to pound the rim back into shape and limp into the next town where you can buy a replacement rim.

Other repairs are far less likely, but they can't be ignored. It is a good idea to carry cone wrenches on long tours. You will probably never overhaul hubs on the road, but you may need to tighten front-wheel cones knocked loose in a crash. Make sure your cone wrenches are the right size for your hubs—with luck, you'll need just two double-ended cone wrenches.

Carry the wrenches necessary to disassemble and overhaul your brakes and derailleurs. These may include 5- and 6-millimeter Allen wrenches and 7-, 8-, 9-, 10-, 11-, and 12-millimeter box wrenches of the stamped steel variety. Occasionally you may need two of any one wrench size, or you may need the odd-size 7-millimeter Allen wrench.

If you have derailleurs that are riveted together and can't be disassembled, a small can of WD-40 or similar penetrating lubricant will restore them after a rainstorm.

Carry the proper tool for your cotterless crankset, the proper chain-link tool for your chain (and a couple of spare links), tools to fit your seat, seatpost, handlebars and stem, and pedals. Some of the before-named Allen wrenches and your trusty six-inch adjustable wrench will work admirably.

It's a great feeling to ride free and independent, knowing that you have a contingency plan to handle any common repair. Only you can decide what tools to take for any particular ride. It all depends on you, your repair skills, and your bike. However, the first time you pull a small, specialized tool out of your pack and get yourself, or a friend, back on the road in minutes, you'll be glad you had the foresight to put together your custom tool kit.

Double-Duty Tools

Up to this point, we've emphasized the importance of acquiring the right tools for the job before you begin working on your bike. Good tools will treat your bike kindly, will make your repair work easier, and will last a long time if you take care of them.

Without taking away from the wisdom of such advice, you have to realize that sometimes the situation requires compromise. It is simply not possible to carry a whole shop full of tools with you every time you set out on your bike. Even on a long tour when you expect to load a fair amount of gear on the bike, there is a limit to how many tools you can or should try to carry.

And having exhausted your savings in buying that special bicycle with the most up-to-date components, you simply may not be able to afford to fully equip your home repair shop right away. So here we offer suggestions on ways you can make up with ingenuity what you lack in specialized equipment.

These ideas come from Andy Di Cyan, a longtime contributor to *Bicycling* magazine. Andy confesses to being at one time a compulsive tool carrier, who used to lug tools that could only be used to fix other people's bikes. Finally, in the interest of traveling light, he began to discover ways to make a given tool

Photograph 1–1. The handle of an adjustable wrench can double as a tire iron.

do a variety of jobs, including some for which it was not intended. Based on his experiences, Andy developed a new way of thinking about tools.

"If you're stuck in the middle of nowhere, alone and with a mechanical problem that looks insoluble, don't panic. Don't think: 'This job needs a tool I don't have, so it can't be done.' Proceed from the point of view that the problem can and will be solved with whatever you can bring to bear on it. Don't think of the tool, think of what needs to be braced, pushed, pulled, or turned here or there, and what you have, or can get, that can do the job. It's the function, not the conventional means of solution, that is your concern; and not why it can't be done, but how it can."

In keeping with this approach, Andy no longer carries tire irons, and claims not to have used them in years. What does he do when a tire needs changing or a tube needs repair? "I remove and remount tires by hand. I pinch the tire all around the rim to move the tire bead from the shoulder of the rim into the

Photograph 1–2. To retain an axle in an emergency, wrap a paper clip around the fork so that it pulls the axle up into the dropout.

well, then I gather all the slack at one point. I work the bead at this point over the rim flange to remove the tire. Occasionally, I run across a rim with an especially high flange or well, a tire with a lot of rubber around the bead, or a thick rim strip, and can't remove it without tools. Then I use the handle of my six-inch adjustable wrench as a tire iron. (Two screwdrivers or bottle openers—used carefully—also work.)"

And here are some more of Andy's unique solutions to on-the-road repair problems.

"What if the nut on your bolt-on hub cracks in the middle of nowhere? Wrap one end of a paper clip (which you've secreted in your patch kit or handlebars) around the end of the axle, twist the clip securely with a Vise-Grip, and fasten the other end to the fork blade in such a way that the wire pulls the axle securely up into the dropout. Use some leather, chamois, or tire patch to protect the paint. Used properly, a Vise-Grip won't damage the finish on your bike, and as we'll see, it can take the place of many tools you'd otherwise need to carry. Brake or gear cable, or a spoke will work in place of a paper clip.

"What if one of your chain's side plates comes off the rivet during a ride when your chain tool is nestled comfortably in your toolbox at home? A six-inch Vise-Grip can remount the plate and put things where they should be.

"You're leaving a building, and a door slams against and breaks the indicator chain on your 3-speed hub. Do you shrink from the prospect of laboring home in highest gear? Pull out what remains of the indicator chain so that the internal sliding clutch comes to where it gives you a low or medium gear. Slide a safety pin or a length of cable through the chain where it exits the long right-hand nut to hold it out and retain that lower gear. If you can't get a safety pin, borrow a few strands of brake or gear cable from the length extending past the fastening nut.

"There you are, routinely applying the brakes or changing gears, and without warning, the barrel or mushroom end your lever bears against separates from the cable. What to do? Unfasten the cable at the other end and pull a length out at the broken end. Take your Vise-Grip and tie a knot as close to the end as possible. Pull the knot tight (two knots may be necessary for a brake cable). Replace the cable, fitting the knot into the lever where the mushroom or barrel end was. For brakes, this should hold at least until you get home. For many gear cables, it's a permanent solution.

"A Vise-Grip or good-quality adjustable wrench serves admirably as a spoke wrench in a pinch. But be sure to keep the tool tight on the flats of the spoke nipple to avoid rounding off the nipple, which is not at all difficult to do. When a nipple does become round and your spoke wrench will no longer turn it, your Vise-Grip probably will.

"If you're blessed with sidepull brakes that lack centering flats (or the flats are inaccessible), centering the calipers can be a real chore. You don't want to trust to divine luck and hope the calipers will center at the same time as you tighten the brake bolt. Lock your Vise-Grip on the raised circular portion of the bolt—the part that holds the spring. Then rotate the calipers gently with the Vise-Grip to your exact satisfaction. This works even though the end fixing nut has been tightened fully on the brake bolt.

"By now you've figured out that I always carry my six-inch Vise-Grip. A good place for yours is under your saddle, fastened with a rubber band to a spare inner tube. Securely tied to the saddle wires with rubber bands or strips of inner tube, it'll be there when you need it. The paper clip and safety pin mentioned earlier can be carried inside the handlebars or taped under the saddle. And if you carry an adjustable wrench, you can wrap it up with your Vise-Grip."

You don't have to agree with all of his solutions to appreciate the resourcefulness with which Andy approaches bicycle repair problems. Equip yourself with a few simple tools and an open mind, and following his example, approach emergency repairs with a positive attitude. Mental resourcefulness can easily be the difference between an aborted trip and an enjoyable tour resumed after a short delay.

Bicycle Aikido

Years ago there was an old newsreel that showed four hulking, young football players trying to push over a 70-year-old Japanese black-belt aikido master. The football players lined up one behind the other and heaved with all their might, but for all they accomplished they could have been trying to push down a tree. The old master stood, leaning toward them, swaying slightly with the changing forces, smiling, and evidently enjoying himself.

Sometimes when you work on your bike, you may feel that you're struggling against forces equal to that of four young football players. Seemingly simple tasks such as removing a wheel may end with the bike, and perhaps you, sprawled on the ground as if you had been gang tackled. You don't have enough hands to hold the bike, the wheel, wrenches, brake spreaders, and what have you all at once. Suddenly, they all gang up on you, and when the play is over, you've lost a couple of yards and are ready to punt.

To avoid such embarrassments, be like the aikido master and learn how to control the bike when you work on it, instead of being overwhelmed by it. There's no great mystery about this; it's only a question of learning how to place your body and how to hold the bicycle and the tools for maximum efficiency. These techniques are especially helpful for roadside repairs when you don't have a repair stand.

Removing and Replacing Wheels

Removing and replacing wheels can be a frustrating experience, especially when you can't flip the bike over onto its handlebars and seat (when touring with tons of stuff on the bike, for example). But a few deft moves and a correct stance will make the job much easier.

When removing a front wheel, stand in front of the bike, facing it. Make sure that the brake calipers clear the tire and rim; release the brake's quick-release lever, if there is one. If there isn't, let the air out of the tire, or remove a brake shoe if necessary.

Loosen the wheel's quick-release or axle nuts, but do not remove the nuts completely; this only makes replacing the wheel more difficult later. Grasp the handlebars with your left hand and the tire with your right hand. Lift the bike off the wheel and lay the bike down on its left side. With practice, you'll do all this in one sweeping motion.

If the bike is carrying a load on its rear rack, it may lean to the right by itself, but in this case, the panniers will protect the drivetrain, and it is all right to lay the bike on its right side. If the bike is carrying an unwieldy load, it may help to grip the wheel between your knees and grasp the handlebars with both hands to gain control of the bike, before removing the wheel.

To replace the front wheel, reverse this process. First make sure that the brake is open or the tire uninflated. Check that the hub's axle nuts or quick-release are loose so the wheel will slide into the dropouts. Then stand in front of the bike (facing it), hold the wheel with one hand and lower the bike onto the wheel axle with the other. Place your head in line with the wheel so you can see each end of the axle and guide the dropouts into place. If your hub has a nutted (non-quick-release) axle, make sure that the washers under the nuts are at the outside of the dropouts; their purpose is to protect the dropouts from the nuts. Don't forget to tighten the nuts with a wrench.

A rear wheel is more of a challenge because of the chain and sprockets. To remove a rear wheel, first open the brake's quick-release, let the air out of the tire, or remove a brake shoe, as you would with a front tire. Next, shift the chain onto the smallest sprocket to increase the clearance to the derailleur. Walk around the bike and loosen the axle nuts or quick-release. Do not remove the axle nuts completely; this only makes replacing the wheel more difficult later.

Now stand to the left of the rear wheel, reach over the bicycle with your left hand, and hold the bike by the right seatstay. Lean the saddle against your belly. It helps to have the cranks horizontal, with the left crank facing forward, to get them out of your way. Pull the rear derailleur body toward the back of the bicycle with your right hand to move it away from the sprockets. At the same time, lift the bike with your left hand.

The wheel should simply fall free. Sometimes, it needs a nudge forward from your right knee. Once the wheel is out, lift and tilt the bike to its left so the chain will clear the wheel. Lay the bike on its left side to protect the derailleur.

To replace the rear wheel, first make sure that the rear derailleur is shifted to the high gear (outside) position. Again, it helps to have the left crank facing forward. Lift the back of the bike with your left hand, place the wheel approximately into position, and lay the upper run of chain over the smallest sprocket ahead of the derailleur. A common mistake is to allow the lower run of chain to rest on top of the sprocket. Remember, the sprockets must be between the upper and lower runs of chain. You can usually position the chain and sprockets by maneuvering the bike, without touching the chain.

Pull the derailleur back with your right hand and slip the wheel into the dropouts. This is easy if all of the parts are

Photograph 1–3. Wheel removal is easy if you stand on the left and grasp the right seatstay with your left hand. Pull the derailleur back with your right hand and lift the bicycle off the wheel.

correctly positioned. The wheel rests on the ground, and you lower the bicycle onto it.

If the dropout spacing does not match the axle, or if nuts and washers are crooked, getting the axle to slide into the dropouts may be a little bit more difficult. Still, as soon as you've got the axle at the front of the dropouts, you can set the bicycle down on the wheel and walk around to the side to push and pry with both hands.

Centering a Wheel

Once you have installed a rear wheel, you must center it. If your bike has axle stops, a one-time adjustment will take care of centering. But many bikes do not have axle stops; you must center the wheel by hand every time you replace it.

On a bike with axle nuts, first tighten the right axle nut. Then crouch at the left side of the bike, just behind the bottom bracket. Wedge your left thumb and index finger between the chainstays and the tire to center it. Now you do not have to look at the tire while you tighten the left axle nut or quick-release using your right hand. Check the centering by standing behind the bike and eyeballing the alignment of the wheel against the seatpost.

The procedure just described is for a derailleur-geared bike whose chain is held taut by a spring in the rear derailleur. On a 1-speed or 3-speed, the adjustment is more complicated because you must adjust the chain so it has a slight amount of slack. If it is too tight, it will put a heavy strain on the bearings in the bottom bracket and rear hub; if it is too loose, it will fall off.

There's a trick to adjusting the chain, which works even with the bicycle resting on its wheels. Pull the rear wheel back in the dropouts until the chain is tight. Then tighten the right axle nut just a little, leaving the left axle nut loose. Slowly turn the crankarms backward while you tap lightly on the midpoint of the upper run of chain with your wrench. This will slip the wheel forward and loosen the chain. To test whether the adjustment is correct, hold the wrench down against the midpoint of the chain while continuing to rotate the crank. Since no chainwheel is perfectly centered on its axle, the chain's slack will vary with crank position. As you turn the crank, the chain should always dip at least three-eighths of an inch where you press on it with the wrench.

Once you have adjusted the chain, finish tightening the right axle nut. Then go to the left side of the bike, center the wheel, and tighten the left axle nut. If the wheel was far off center, the chain may be thrown slightly out of adjustment. If so, loosen the right axle nut partway and readjust the chain

Photograph 1–4. To center a rear wheel, crouch to the left and wedge your left thumb and index finger between the tire and chainstays and center the tire, then tighten the axle nut or quick-release.

slack. Repeat the sequence until the wheel is centered and the chain slack is correct. Loosen one axle nut at a time, never both. This way, the wheel will move closer and closer to the position you want; you'll "walk" the wheel into position, always adjusting the right side to set the chain slack or the left side to center the wheel between the chainstays.

Sometimes, the simplest way to deal with a problem is to go around it. For example, you can release one side of the tire from the rim and get a punctured tube out enough to patch it while the wheel remains on the bicycle. Since you then won't have to adjust the chain, this becomes a much more convenient way to deal with a flat on the rear wheel of a 3-speed or 1-speed bicycle. You only need to remove the wheel if you are going to replace the inner tube or tire.

Replacing a Tire

Installing a tire onto a rim requires a special technique all its own. It is easiest if you have let all the air out of the tube. The first side of the tire is easy to get on. The second side can usually be slipped into place without tools, unless you have an unusually tight tire/rim combination. (For these tight combinations, you'll need a tire lever for the last several inches.) Tuck the tire into place at the valve first so that the valve doesn't get pinched. Spin the wheel so that the valve is at the bottom. Now, beginning at the valve, work the left and right sides of the bead into place around the rim at the same time, using both hands. When your hands meet at the top, hook your fingers over the far side of the rim and push on the tire bead with your two thumbs together. The combined force of your finger squeezing and thumb pushing will pop the bead over the rim.

Conquering Pedals

Once you have a pedal started onto the threads of the crank when installing it, screwing it on can be sped up by turning the cranks backward while holding the wrench still. But using a wrench to tighten or loosen a pedal can be a real pain if it merely turns the crank instead. This problem is most annoying when you don't have a repair stand or a mechanic's long pedal wrench—when you're in an airport where you must remove the pedals to box your bike, for example.

A simple trick makes the job easier. Turn the crank so it faces forward, then the chain will prevent the crank from turning. To tighten a pedal, fit the wrench so it sticks out beyond the end of the crank and push down. This will work on either pedal since the left pedal tightens counterclockwise. The orientation of the crank may vary a bit since the flats of the pedal may line up at any angle, but you will always be able to get the crank facing more or less forward.

To loosen a pedal, face the crank forward but position the wrench as much as possible next to the crank, pointing in toward the crank spindle, then push down. You can even push with your foot to loosen a stubborn pedal. When loosening a pedal, it is best if you can get the wrench horizontal and below the level of the bottom bracket. One exception: if you have an extra-long wrench that extends past the crank spindle, you will need to grip the wrench at its midpoint (or inboard of the spindle) or hold the pedal still with your other hand.

Another way to get extra leverage on a pedal is to place the wrench near the crank so you can wrap your hands around both and squeeze them together like the handles of a pair of pliers. Be careful not to get your fingers between the two or you may jam them when the pedal begins to turn.

This list could go on indefinitely because there are tricks and methods of dealing with every part of your bike. As you work with your bike, you'll discover many mechanics' tricks, based on an understanding of physical principles and of how to use your strength effectively. Once you learn how to physically work with your bike, you will realize that even you can gain control over a heavily laden, stubborn bicycle. So be like the aikido master—use your wits and your opponent's strength to further your own goals. Your bicycle will work with you when you work with it.

A Simple Tool Bag

How do you keep your tools handy when you are on the road? How do you avoid leaving a tool at home or losing it along the way? With a tool bag, of course.

Go to your bike shop, and you will see that there are a lot of commercially made bags to choose from. The best ones, in our opinion, are those that completely enclose their contents. Such bags protect tires or tubes from light, moisture, and air (which can cause rubber to crack) and eliminate the possibility of anything falling out. We've found that bags equipped with Velcro strips are the easiest to open and close.

But perhaps you want to be creative, you carry some exotic tools, or you just want to save a few dollars and make your own tool bag. If so, you should consider a traditional roll up type of bag like the one featured here.

Our tool roll is made of heavy cloth and has separate pockets for various tools and spare parts. It organizes tools and prevents them from being misplaced. Spread the roll open and you can tell at a glance if all your tools are there. It will also keep your tools protected and keep them from clanking and bashing against one another or against other gear in your pack. This type of bag is useful for both an extensive cross-country tour or just an afternoon's outing.

You will need the following materials: a piece of heavy fabric, like denim, approximately 17 × 18 inches (these are the measurements of the one that we made; however, you can custom size your own); heavy thread; 44 inches of ¼-inch-wide cloth tape (or you can use a strip cut from the fabric).

To make your own bag, first set out all the tools you want to travel with. Lay the tools out parallel to each other with about one inch of space between them. Small tools, such as a chain tool and a spoke wrench, can be placed together. Each tool or group will be in its own separate pocket. You can make a large pocket for miscellaneous items.

Measure the length and the height of the area taken up by the tools. Add two inches to the length. Double the height and add three inches. This is the size of the piece of fabric you will need. Jot down the widths of each tool pocket you will want.

Hem the piece of fabric on all sides. Fold it along its length so the two edges are parallel and three inches apart. Stitch each of the tool pockets to the widths you have recorded. We recommend double-stitching all seams. You may leave more fabric on either side of the pockets—making the roll longer than necessary—thereby creating a softer roll.

To make the ties, take the cloth tape or the strip of fabric and fold it in half. Sew the fold securely near one edge in the middle of an end pocket. This completes your tool roll. For a more contemporary touch, buy a short length of Velcro, cut it into two pieces, and sew them to the roll where appropriate.

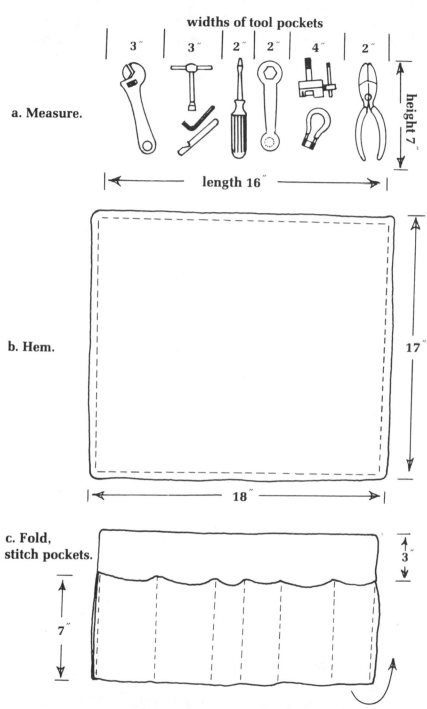

Illustration 1–2. Size this roll-up bag for your own set of tools.

To use your new roll, place your tools in the pockets and fold down the top edge over the openings of the pockets. Roll toward the side with the ties and wrap the ties around the roll and knot. Tie the bag securely to the underside or back of your seat, and you are ready to travel.

Part Two
Bottom Bracket Repairs

Bottom Bracket Adjustment

Adjusting bottom bracket bearings is similar to adjusting wheel bearings but slightly more complicated. With wheel bearing cones, tightening the locknut presses on the cone so that the bearing adjustment becomes slightly tighter than it was before you tightened the locknut. But when you tighten the lockring on the adjustable cup of a conventional bottom bracket, the bearing adjustment will sometimes become tighter, sometimes looser!

As the locknut pushes against the edge of the bottom bracket shell, it pulls the adjustable cup outward just a little bit. When this is all that happens, the bearings get looser. But sometimes, as you tighten the lockring, the friction of the threads will cause the adjustable cup to turn with the lockring—in this case, the adjustment will become tighter. You cannot tell which way it will go on a particular bicycle until you try it.

Bottom bracket bearings are much more heavily stressed than wheel bearings and are more difficult to adjust to the perfect balance between looseness and tightness. To adjust a bottom bracket, first adjust the bearings to be clearly too loose. Revolve the spindle slowly with your fingertips—do not roll your fingertips around the spindle but revolve it by turning your wrist. Your fingers should stay in constant light contact with the spindle.

Pretend you are turning the knob of a safe, trying to feel the tumblers drop in. Turn it for several complete revolutions in both directions. It should not have any roughness or un-

Photograph 2–1. A bottom bracket with crankarms removed.

evenness at any point. If it does, that is a sign that the spindle, cups, or balls are damaged or that there is dirt in the bearing. Make a mental note of how easily the spindle turns when the bearing is too loose—it should turn just as freely when you have finished adjusting it.

Bearing play is checked by trying to rock the end of the spindle up and down. Ideally, there should be no play at all, but in almost all cases, if you eliminate the play completely, the bearings will bind. If in doubt, it is better to have the bearings just a bit too loose than too tight. In our experience, only

Campagnolo bottom brackets can be adjusted for no play and still turn as freely as they should.

Don't try to judge the adjustment of bottom bracket bearings until the lockring has been securely tightened. If you are adjusting a bottom bracket that is tending to rotate the cup with the lockring, you may be tempted to hold the cup stationary with a pin tool—this is not a good idea because it can put excessive stress on the pins of the pin tool. It is better in such cases to allow the cup to rotate and make use of a little "Kentucky windage."

In cases where the cup tends to turn with the lockring, the bearing adjustment will become tighter when the lockring is tightened securely. If it becomes too tight, loosen the lockring and cup together. Turn the lockring clockwise on the cup, then retighten the lockring and cup as a unit until secure. Recheck the bearing adjustment. If it is still too tight, repeat this procedure. If it is too loose, loosen both pieces together. Turn the lockring counterclockwise just a bit and retighten both pieces together.

If, on the other hand, the lockring of the bicycle you are working on can be tightened without tending to turn the adjustable cup, you must first adjust the cup so that the bearings are too tight, then tighten the lockring. The lockring will pull the adjustable cup out just a bit. If you have judged correctly, the bearings will then be properly adjusted.

Educate Your Hands

Either way, it is a process of trial and error. With practice, you can learn to get the adjustment right after just a couple of tries, but this requires that you "educate" your hands. If you have not done this job many times, you should expect to have to keep loosening the lockring and readjusting the bearings as many as five to ten times before you have it right.

Take your time and be patient. As you approach the ideal adjustment, the corrections will need to be made just a couple of degrees at a time. Judging the adjustment is basically the same as with wheel bearings—perfection consists in having no play and no friction. Perfection is, of course, elusive, so the best you can hope for is to minimize both.

Bearing Installation and Maintenance

When you take a bottom bracket apart to repack it, there are a couple of other things that you can do to keep your bike happy. One is to spray LPS-3 or some similar treatment up into the tubes and chainstays to retard rust. Another is to make sure that the bearings are protected from contamination by one of the special plastic sleeves made for the purpose. You can cut your own liners from tin cans or plastic jugs for this, but the accordion-type sleeves made for the purpose give a much superior seal, and they are quite inexpensive.

Do not think that you don't need a bottom bracket sleeve just because you have a closed seatpost! Although open seatposts on bikes without mudguards are the leading cause of dirty bottom brackets, even the cleanest, most carefully made bike is likely to have leftover brazing flux, paint chips, or other debris inside its frame tubes. All of this will eventually wind up in your bottom bracket.

Most newer bicycles come with "caged" bearing balls—the balls are held in metal or plastic retainers. This makes it easier to install the balls but usually at a cost in performance. A standard three-piece-type bottom bracket takes 11 loose ¼-inch balls per side. Most retainers hold fewer balls, so each ball and its contact point with the cup and cone are more heavily stressed. This causes higher friction and more rapid wear.

If your bottom bracket came with retainers holding fewer than 11 balls, we strongly recommend that you replace them with loose balls. This is not really difficult to do if you know how.

The frame should be lying on its right side, with the fixed cup and liner installed. Squirt plenty of grease into both cups. Set 11 balls into the adjustable cup. Drop the shorter end of the spindle into the cup, and it will hold the balls in place even if you are using a thin grease. Holding the adjustable cup and spindle as a unit, turn them over so that the cup is on top. Set this assembly aside in this position, supported by the spindle. (A convenient place to put it temporarily is into the right crank; the chainwheel will prevent it from falling over.)

Next, stick a finger up through the hole in the fixed cup to keep the balls from falling through. Drop 11 balls down into the cup and arrange them in a circle around your finger. Then, pick up the spindle (with the adjustable cup already installed) and lower it down until it rests on the finger that is sticking up through the fixed cup. Lower it farther, until you can begin to screw the adjustable cup into the bottom bracket threads. Keep the spindle supported from below until the adjustable cup is screwed well in because if you release the spindle while the cup is very loose, the balls may fall out of position.

Don't try to reuse some of the balls from your retainer—it is very important that all of the balls in a race be from the same production lot so that they will all be the same size. Good-quality bearing balls from a given lot will usually be within 2 or 3 millionths of an inch of each other in size, but if you mix lots, the difference can easily be 25 or 30 millionths. If there is this much difference in size, the smaller ones might just as well be missing for all the good they will do!

Cotter Pin Removal and Installation

Does one of the bikes in your family fleet have cottered cranks? And have you delayed servicing its bottom bracket because you hesitate to deal with the challenge of removing a cotter pin? Cotter pin removal does take some effort, but there are a number of possible methods by which it can be done. The tried and true method, employed by the majority of bike mechanics, is to drive the pin out using a hammer and punch. Here is how it is done.

First, loosen the cotter nut to the point of being flush with the outer end of the cotter pin so you'll have a large, even surface on which to hammer. It is a good idea to support the crank with a block of wood to absorb much of the force of the

Illustration 2–1. Removing a cotter pin using a hammer and drift punch. Note the grooved wooden block used to support the crank.

hammer blows. Cut a piece of 4 × 4 to approximately 11 inches in length and either notch or drill a hole in one end to receive the pin as it exits the crank. Using a punch, hammer gently on the nut so as not to damage its threads. Hammer as long as necessary until the cotter loosens. Remove the nut and washer. Drive the cotter the rest of the way out.

When reassembling the cranks, reverse the process, but install a new cotter pin rather than try to reuse the old one. Cotter pins are inexpensive and not worth trying to salvage after removal. Every 50 miles for the next 250 miles, give the new pin a sharp tap with the hammer and tighten the nut. After this 250-mile treatment, cotters can be expected to stay tight.

But perhaps you shrink from banging cotter pins with a hammer to get them on and off, and fear that a wooden block won't really protect your bearing cups from hammer blows. Maybe you are not skilled enough with a hammer to drive a new pin in place without mushrooming its head. And even

Photograph 2–2. A cottered crankset.

though there are cotter pin presses made by bike tool manufacturers, which will do the job properly, you cannot afford their price. If so, then you may wish to try one of the following alternative methods.

Vise-Grip adjustable locking pliers will do the job nonviolently and do it as well as the commercially made pin press tools. To remove a cotter pin that's been in place for some time, it is advisable first, after removing the nut and washer, to drip some penetrating oil into the junction between pin and crank and let it work overnight.

Next morning, take your large (ten-inch or larger) curved-jaw Vise-Grip, adjust the jaws so that when open they barely clear the distance to be spanned, and apply it so that one jaw bears on the threaded end of the cotter pin and the other on

Photograph 2–3. A cotter pin pressed into place by a Vise-Grip. Press on the threaded end of the pin to remove it.

the body of the crank. Squeeze the handle and lock the tool. It will then be pushing the threaded end through and out of the crank. If the pin does not pop out, release the locking lever, screw down the jaw adjuster a bit, and again lock it to bear against the threaded end of the cotter. Repeat as necessary until the pin pops out or until you cannot lock the tool at a higher force. In the latter case, with the jaws locked and bearing hard on the threaded end, tap the sides of the pin and crankarm with a mallet.

The above approach works well when dealing with frozen cotters, and usually neither the oil nor the mallet is necessary. Should your cotter be truly stubborn, leave it overnight with the Vise-Grip bearing on the threaded end at as high a force as you can lock it. Generally it will fall out during the night.

Installing a cotter pin with a Vise-Grip is similar to removing one but less dramatic. Here's how to do it.

1. Obtain new cotters of the correct size for the spindle and crank.
2. Paint the pin's flat surface with an indelible felt-tip marker.
3. Press the pin into the crank with the Vise-Grip, one jaw bearing against the large end, the other against the crank. The threaded ends of the pin should point down when the crank is in the forward position, a configuration least likely to snag clothing or shoelaces.
4. Remove the pin, using the Vise-Grip.
5. Examine the pin's flat surface and file it a bit where the marker's pigment is worn off.
6. Repeat steps 2 through 5 until the pigment on the flat is worn evenly.
7. Before installing the pin for the last time, coat its surface with grease or antiseize compound. Repeat step 3.
8. Screw down the jaw adjuster slightly and repeat step 3.
9. Repeat step 8 until you cannot push the pin any farther.
10. Apply some thread-locking compound to the threads of the cotter, slip on the washer, and fasten the nut firmly.

If you followed these instructions carefully, your cotter pins should be secure. Nevertheless, you might want to check them after you have ridden your bike 50 miles or so. Apply pressure to the pins one more time to see if they will go farther into the cranks, then snug the nuts. After this, they should remain tight until the next time you need to remove them for bottom bracket maintenance.

Removing and Installing Cotterless Cranks

Aluminum alloy cotterless cranks have replaced steel cottered cranks on all but the least expensive bicycles. The advantages of lighter weight, easier maintenance, and closer dimensional tolerances have made cotterless cranks very popular. Manufacturers have perfected ways of making cotterless cranksets so that today's cheaper models hardly cost any more than the cottered cranks they have replaced.

One drawback of cotterless cranks is that their installation and removal require special tools, unlike cottered cranks, which can be installed and removed with common tools like hammers and Vise-Grip pliers. However, cotterless crank tools are easy to use, requiring less skill than the tools used to work on cottered cranks. They are also small and light, weighing only a few ounces. Thus, they can more easily be carried on the road than tools needed for cottered cranks.

To install or adjust cotterless cranks, you need a socket-type wrench known as a crankarm bolt spanner or spindle bolt spanner. To remove a cotterless crank from its spindle, you need a crank puller to fit your brand of crank. The crankarm bolt spanner and crank puller are often sold together in a small tool kit.

To better understand this repair procedure, let's look at how a cotterless crank is secured to its spindle. The ends of the spindle are square in cross section and are slightly tapered to make them narrower at their tips. There is a corresponding tapered square hole in the crank. Depending on the brand and model, the crank is secured on its spindle by either a bolt or a nut. Generally these two crank spindle designs are refered to as Type I and Type II.

Type I is the older, more traditional design. It employs a hollow spindle threaded to receive a bolt, commonly called the crankarm fixing bolt. A flat washer under the bolt head completes the system. The Type II crank design uses a spindle with a small threaded stud protruding past the ends of the square, tapered section. A nut threads onto this stud to secure the crank

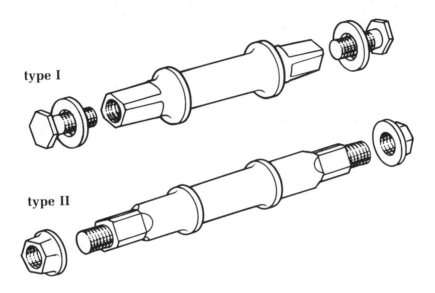

type I

type II

Illustration 2–2. Type I cranksets have a hollow spindle threaded to
receive a bolt. Type II cranksets use a spindle with a stud threaded
to receive a nut.

on the spindle. Usually, the nut is a special nut with a serrated
face so that no separate washer is required.

Removing a Cotterless Crank

The first step in removing a cotterless crank is to remove
the dust cap, if any. Depending on the brand, this is unscrewed
either with a five-millimeter Allen wrench or with a wide-blade
screwdriver. Don't use a small srewdriver, as you run the risk
of damaging the slot—most dust caps are soft aluminum or
plastic. If you don't have a wide-blade screwdriver, a cone wrench
or a dime will often fit nicely.

Photograph 2–4. The first step in removing a cotterless crank is to remove the dust cap. Do so carefully.

Next, remove the fixing bolt or nut that holds the crank to the axle. Since the bolt or nut is recessed inside a cavity in the crank, you need a thin-walled socket or a crankarm bolt spanner to turn it. If a nut is used, it will be 14 millimeters. If a bolt is used, it will usually have a 15-millimeter head; Stronglight and Zeus use 16-millimeter bolts. Be especially careful to remove any washers that may be present, or you may easily destroy the dust cap threads inside the crankarm by trying to push the crank puller rod against the washer.

Now you are ready to use the crank puller. This tool is a joy to use and with reasonable care will work every time with no complications. A cotterless crank puller is made up of two parts that function like a nut and a bolt. The "nut" is a cylinder bearing both male and female threads as well as flats for a wrench. This cylinder threads onto the bolt-like base of the puller like a nut and screws into the dust cap threads of the crankarm like a bolt.

Before you begin to screw the crank puller cylinder into the dust cap threads, back the base of the puller out of the way. Otherwise, it will hit the end of the spindle and prevent the cylinder from penetrating the entire threaded area of the crankarm, and it is important that it be screwed in as far as possible. The dust cap threads will be subjected to severe stress as the crank is removed, so the more contact there is between them and the puller, the less chance there will be of stripping them. But don't overtighten the cylinder either. Most of the time you should not need to use a wrench on it and can easily tell when you have gone far enough.

If you must use a wrench, handle it with a light touch and stop when you have reached the end of the dust cap threads. Any further turning will only do harm to the threads.

Once the puller cylinder is securely screwed into the crank, turn the head of the bolt clockwise to send it through the cylinder until it makes contact with the end of the spindle. Rotate the bolt further to draw the crank off the spindle. Usually, the crank will fall off in your hand with surprisingly little effort because of the very high mechanical advantage of the tool. On some less expensive "melt-forged" cranks, considerably more force may be needed to break the crank free from its spindle.

Buy the Tool You Need

Which tool to buy depends on what brand and model of crankset you have. Although most types of cranksets use the same one-thread-per-millimeter pitch, there are three common diameters for the dust cap threads: Campagnolo, 22 millimeter; T.A., 22.8 millimeter; and Stronglight, 23 millimeter. So far as we know, all other brands use the same size as Campagnolo.

To service a T.A. crankset, you need a T.A. puller. For Stronglight, ideally, you should have a Stronglight puller, but the T.A. is usable (although it fits a bit more loosely than it should). For any other brand, you have a wider choice available.

Here are some things to keep in mind as you shop among the alternatives.

Pullers made primarily for Type I cranksets usually have a rotating collar on the end of the "bolt." This collar is the part that actually pushes against the end of the spindle to pull the crank off. If you use this type of tool on a Type II spindle, it will work sometimes, though the threaded stud on the end of the spindle may prevent the tool from engaging the dust cap threads completely. Some Type I pullers simply don't fit on Type II cranksets.

Of the tools intended for Type II spindles, the Sugino Maxy crank puller is particularly nice; it includes its own spindle bolt spanner. It can be used with a six-inch or larger adjustable wrench or a 14-millimeter open-end wrench. The Maxy puller has a dome-shaped end to push against the male threaded stud on Type II spindles. When this tool is used with a Type I female threaded spindle, the sides of the "bolt" of the puller rub against the edges of the spindle threads that the crank bolts screw into. There is a slight possibility that the spindle threads could be damaged by this, but bottom bracket spindles are made of such very hard steel that the risk is small.

Park's Universal Puller

The closest thing to a universal crank puller is made by Park. This has a reversible, double-ended "nut," with T.A. threads on one end and Campagnolo threads on the other end. The wrench flats are in the middle. The "bolt" of this tool is even more unusual than the "nut." It has its own wrench welded onto one end, and the other end has a special contour so that it works well with either Type I or Type II threaded spindles.

If you want to be able to service the greatest variety of cranksets with the minimum number of tools, the Park puller is the one to buy. If you are concerned only with being able to service the particular type on your own bicycle, the tool made by the crank manufacturer is a better choice. It will be lighter in weight and will provide a better fit than the Park tool.

There are several types of crankarm bolt spanners suitable for removing and reinstalling the crank fixing bolt (or nut). The crank manufacturers all make small, easily carried spanners with single-size sockets to fit their fixing bolts. Park makes a very well-thought-out "universal" crankarm bolt spanner with 14-, 15-, and 16-millimeter sockets on a handle that is just short enough to clear the pedal on most cranksets. One end of this wrench is designed to serve as a screwdriver for the dust caps, and there is also a short 5-millimeter Allen wrench built in for those dust caps that require one. This wrench is also very handy for general use—for axle nuts, seatpost bolts, and other parts.

Alternative Tools

For shop use, many mechanics prefer to use an automotive-type socket wrench with a ratchet handle instead of the specialized tools we have been describing. This works very well, but you must be careful not to overtighten crankarm fixing bolts or nuts when using a wrench with an unusually long handle. Also, if you wish to use this type of wrench, you may have some difficulty finding sockets that are the right size for the bolt but have a small enough outside diameter to fit inside the dust cap threads.

Most likely this will not be a problem for a 14-millimeter socket, but many 15- and 16-millimeter sockets are too thick. It's legendarily difficult to get the 16-millimeter bolt out of the smaller Campagnolo-size dust cap hole on a Zeus crankset. The Zeus tool works, but very few other tools do.

Usually the better quality sockets will have thinner walls—cheap sockets try to make up for poor quality steel by having more of it. Sockets come in 6-point and 12-point types. Six-point sockets tend to have slightly thinner walls, so they are more likely to fit. For use with ratchets, 6-point sockets are preferable anyway because of the better contact with the nut that they provide. You should also note that ⅜-inch drive sockets tend to be thinner than ½-inch drive sockets.

Cranks That Need No Puller

One promising development is the crankset that needs no puller. Shimano introduced the first such crankset several years ago with its One-Key Release system. More recently, Excel and Sugino began offering similar units. All work the same way. Instead of the customary 15-millimeter bolt, these cranksets use a bolt with a 6-millimeter Allen head. This has two advantages:

the necessary tool is small and practically weightless, and the Allen head can be exposed through a small hole in the dust cap.

The steel dust cap in this system fulfills the function of the "nut" on a standard crank puller, and when you're removing the crank, the fixing bolt fills the role of the crank puller's "bolt." As you loosen the fixing bolt, the head of the bolt pushes against the inside of the dust cap, pulling the crank from the spindle.

This system is particularly well-suited for touring and for air travel when you need to remove either the pedals or the cranks to put your bicycle into a box. You can adapt other brands of cranks to this system by replacing the dust caps and fixing bolts. Shimano, Excel, and Sugino all offer retrofit kits. They will work with all Type I cranks (that use a bolt to hold the crank to the spindle) with Campagnolo-size (22-millimeter) dust cap threads. A notable drawback of the design is that cranks so easily removed invite theft.

Photograph 2–5. The bolts in some of the newer cranksets are removed with an Allen wrench instead of a crank puller.

Installing Cranks

Most people install cranks by slapping them onto the spindle, tightening the fixing bolt until it feels about right, and throwing the dust cap away. While this method usually works, there are drawbacks to it. For one thing, the dust cap is important. It protects the crankarm threads from all sorts of possible abuse. Also, the tapers on your crank spindle may need lubrication to ease the tightening of the crankarms. Unfortunately, there is much disagreement among experts concerning this and the amount of torque one should apply to the fixing bolts.

The traditional argument against lubricating the tapers is that lubrication allows you to overtighten the fixing bolt and stretch the hole in the crankarm. On the other side, the argument in favor of lubricating the tapers is that it helps prevent corrosion, fusing, and galling, and facilitates removal.

What this debate overlooks is that some cranks may need lubrication whereas others do not. It's easy to get an expensive, high-quality crankset to work properly without lubrication, but the less-expensive cranksets often creak and groan no matter how much one tightens the fixing bolts. Lubricating the tapers can stop this noise.

Another benefit of lubrication for less-expensive cranksets is that they have case-hardened steel spindles and lower-quality anodization of their aluminum crankarms. These surfaces readily oxidize unless they're protected by a lubricant/moisture barrier. In general, we would say that Type I cranksets, since they are usually high quality, do not need a lubricant, while Type II do. As for the lubricant you use, grease, antiseize compounds, and oil all have their advocates. The differences among them are less important than the difference between lubrication and no lubrication.

Lubricate Threads

Regardless of the quality of your crankset, you should lubricate the threads of the fixing bolt (or nut) and both surfaces of the washer that sits under the bolt head (if you have such a washer). Recommended torque varies with the brand of crankset used and with the outcome of the lube/don't lube decision.

Ask a knowledgeable mechanic what is preferred for your components.

Also, remember that when you lubricate the tapers, you need to lower the torque drastically, or you'll overtighten the fixing bolt. Many people report that overtightening plus lubrication can deform the crankarm. Somewhere around five to nine foot-pounds is said to be correct for lubricated torque.

If you have a Type II spindle, you have a built-in defense against overtightening. In our experience, the nuts used to hold the crankarms on these spindles will crack before you can overtighten them. Instead of replacing expensive cranks, all you have to do is replace inexpensive nuts.

With all these differing recommendations and bits of conflicting advice, what should you do? Many reasonable people will disagree with our advice, but here it is—try it dry. If it creaks, ride/retighten, ride/retighten to set the crank onto the spindle. If it still creaks, lubricate the tapers. If you have an experienced mechanic's feel for tightening bolts, rely on that. Intuition can sometimes work better than published recommended torque settings.

If you don't have a mechanic's feel, make sure you use a wrench with a handle of eight inches or less; a longer handle makes it too easy to overtighten. Borrow a torque wrench to calibrate your two-grunt heave, or better yet, ask a skilled wrench-waver to look over your shoulder and guide you.

Part Three
Wheel Repairs

A Crash Course in Rim Repair

The spoked bicycle wheel is a fabulous invention. Imagine just a couple of pounds of lightweight metal supporting a couple hundred pounds of bike and rider through all kinds of bumps, bangs, turns, and stresses. But the beautiful engineering of the tensioned wheel isn't indomitable. Accidents are inevitable, and they can and very often do damage or even ruin a wheel.

Fortunately, there is a way to save a wheel that's been bent. With a little work and a little acquired technique, you can learn to straighten a rim that even most bike shop mechanics would relegate to the trash pile. And for accidents that happen away from home, you can almost always straighten a wheel sufficiently to ride it home. Although you can seldom make a damaged wheel good as new, you can often restore it to lengthy service.

First, the problem. When a wheel is stressed from the side (as when cornering), the tension of the spokes holds the rim in place and keeps it from bending. In an accident, however, or under severe stress, the rim simply gives way to lateral pressure and instead of flexing slightly, actually bends into a giant potato-chip shape.

Let's say you just took a spill on a back road, ten miles from home. You get up, dust yourself off, and find your only problem is a rim that looks sprung beyond repair. Normally, a spoke wrench would get out small kinks, but this is too serious a bend for that. Time to start the long walk home? Wait a minute.

The solution is to re-create the accident in reverse, and with a little ingenuity, you can do just that. But first, a little

47

wheel-truing theory. In ordinary wheel truing, the rim is pulled into line by loosening or tightening the appropriate spokes. If you know the basics of truing, you also know that only small bends can be taken out this way.

What you may not know, however, is that a perfectly straight rim achieved this way does not mean that a bent wheel has been fixed. Once a rim has been bent and then straightened solely through spoke adjustment, some spokes will be much tighter than others; although the wheel may look fine, it will have no structural integrity at all. The next pothole may collapse it.

In a good wheel, on the other hand, all the spokes will be very nearly under the same tension. The right and left sides of a rear wheel on derailleur bikes are an exception to this rule because each side is tightened to a slightly different tension to produce freewheel dish. However, all the spokes on each side are set to the same value or nearly so.

An important rule to keep in mind is that the technique for straightening wheels usually means using a spoke wrench as little as possible. All too often, cyclists try to fix a bent wheel by using a spoke wrench almost exclusively. Certainly, if a couple of spokes are loose in a wheel, it seems logical to tighten them. But generally, these spokes are loose because the rim is bent, and tightening them will only bend it more in the same direction.

As a rule, when a wheel is bent, the problem is with the rim. The one obvious exception is when a spoke is broken. Then you replace the spoke and your problem is most likely solved. But usually when you bend a wheel, you'll find that no spokes are broken. The rim is bent, and that is what you must straighten.

Thus, to fix a bent wheel, you first have to stress the rim back into as straight a condition as possible and then start truing. Here's how.

With the wheel off the bike, place the bent area of the rim against some solid surface such as a curb, if you are stuck outdoors, or a workbench, if you can get to one. Place the rim so that the bend faces away from you, and put your hands about 20 inches apart, with the bend centered between them. Now push. That's it. You'll feel the rim beginning to straighten. Don't worry about the spokes; they won't break.

Photograph 3–1. Place your hands 20 inches apart, with the bend centered between them, take a deep breath, then push the rim firmly against a solid surface.

The stress you're applying is local and mostly on the rim itself. Spokes work in a system and are not affected by localized stress. The whole operation takes surprisingly little force, although some heavy-duty steel rims will require considerably more pressure to move than an aluminum rim. If you happen to go too far, just turn the wheel over and push the rim back the other way.

With a little fiddling, the wheel will be reasonably straight, and you can then get out the spoke wrench and go to it. You'll have a wheel that will true up much more easily and one with more even spoke tension and greater strength.

A repaired wheel is never quite as good as an undamaged wheel, but with careful work it can be serviceable. And that is a big improvement over having to catch a ride home or limp along for hours until you can get to a bike shop.

When you do get home, take the wheel to a good wheel builder for a professional inspection and, if necessary, repair or replacement of damaged parts.

Changing a Tire

Ever so often, your bike is going to let you down with a flat tire. Chances are it will happen just as you are about to go on a ride with friends or about to leave for your daily commute to work. Don't despair. Once you have mastered the right technique, you can change a flat in less than ten minutes and be on your way.

It doesn't take too much time to learn how to change a flat, and knowing how makes a difference in how much you can enjoy the independence of cycling. After reading these instructions, you should practice changing a tire a few times, for in this endeavor as in most, practice makes perfect.

Your first step is to make sure the tire can fit through the brake shoes so that you can remove the wheel. Normally, you only remove the wheel when the tire is flat, and a flat tire will fit through the brake shoes without any problem. (More expensive bikes have a quick-release mechanism on the brakes so you can fit an inflated tire through them as well.)

Your next step is to get into position to remove the wheel from the bike. Almost any position will work for the front wheel, but the rear wheel can be more confusing. To get ready to remove the rear wheel, shift the derailleurs into the smallest rear cog and the small front chainring, then stand behind the bike.

Loosen the axle nuts or, in the case of better bikes, the quick-release. (You need the proper size wrench to remove axle nuts. A six-inch adjustable wrench is useful since it will fit your friends' bikes, too.)

Now remove the wheel, being careful not to damage or tangle the chain and the rear derailleur, and set the bicycle aside. If it's the rear wheel you removed, use a twig to prop the chain off of the ground. Chains can get amazingly tangled and dirty.

Next you need to remove the tire from the rim. In the best of all worlds, you can do this with your bare hands. Often, you need a set of tire irons. (It depends on the specific tire and rim.) Just don't use a screwdriver—you're likely to puncture the inner tube again.

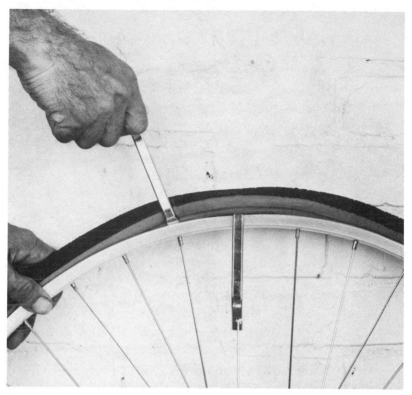

Photograph 3–2. Often a pair of tire irons is needed to remove a tire from its rim.

Select a spot 90 degrees from the valve stem to begin. Call that the "top" of the wheel. Grasp the tire there and pinch the walls of the tire together. Pull upward on the tire there while you take your other hand to the bottom of the wheel. With your other hand, pinch the sidewalls together so they can drop into the deep channel in the center of the rim. The idea is to get as much slack tire as you can at the top.

If you can, push the tire sideways off the rim with your bare hands. If that won't work, use tire irons (the newer plastic tire "irons" are especially nice to use) to flip the tire bead off the edge of the rim. Use a couple of tire irons to flip a greater and greater length of bead off the rim, until the last portion is ready to pop off.

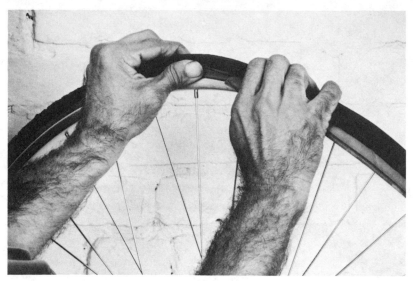

Photograph 3–3. Sometimes you can reassemble a wheel with your bare hands, even if you needed tire irons to take it apart.

With the inner tube still in the tire, find the leak by pumping up the tube and listening for the hiss. Look for broken glass or other debris in the tire near the leak. Use tape to patch any small hole in the tire casing.

Pull the inner tube out of the tire and prepare to patch it by using sandpaper to clean and roughen the inner tube surface surrounding the hole. Coat the roughened surface with patch kit rubber cement and allow the cement to dry.

Remove the protective backing from a patch and press the patch onto the inner tube over the hole. Squeeze so you get good contact between the patch and the tire. Spread talcum powder inside the tire casing so the inner tube doesn't chafe.

Reassemble the wheel, working the tube back inside the tire and fitting the tire back on the rim. (Sometimes a wheel that had to be taken apart with tire irons can be reassembled with your bare hands.) Put the wheel back on the bike, center it in the frame and fasten it in place. Then pump up the tire.

Changing a tire is really not a difficult procedure, but you would be wise to practice doing it in the comfort of your home before you have to do it out on the road.

Repairing Tubular Tires

If you are one of those cyclists who has decided to upgrade your bike by equipping it with a new set of wheels, you may be considering switching to tubular tires. Everyone who has tried them insists that lightweight tubulars furnish a dramatic improvement in handling, acceleration, and deceleration over ordinary clinchers. Although the newer high-pressure, narrow-profile clinchers run a close second and are a better choice for touring and commuting, tubular tires provide ultimate performance for unloaded and fast riding on well-paved roads.

However, along with the advantages offered by tubular tires come disadvantages. One of them is cost. Not only do you have to pay the initial cost of new wheels and tires, but also, because of their shorter life, tubulars will end up costing you nearly twice as much per mile as high-pressure clinchers. Most troublesome of all is the high vulnerability of tubular tires to punctures because of the thinness of their material. And although it is not terribly difficult, repairing a puncture on a tubular is a tedious and time-consuming job, one that can take you three times as long as on any ordinary tire, despite the fact that putting a new tubular tire on your rim is quick.

To repair a punctured tubular, the first thing you'll need is a patch kit specifically for tubular tires. In the kit you'll find a tube of rubber cement, rubber patches of various sizes, and a needle with thread. Some kits include talcum powder; if yours doesn't, simply borrow some from your bathroom. You'll also need pieces of cotton and silk tire casing material and a pair of sharp scissors.

To find the area of the puncture, inflate the tire as best you can and immerse a portion at a time in clean water. When you see a steady stream of bubbles, mark the spot with a ballpoint pen from one sidewall over the seam tape and onto the opposite sidewall.

Beware: the escaping air may mislead you by flowing around inside the casing and bubbling out at some place other than the puncture. If the tire will hold air for a few moments, you can pinpoint the exact location of the leak by putting the tire on a rim and inflating it very tightly. This presses the tube against the casing and restricts the lateral flow of escaping air so that the bubbles emerge near the puncture.

Next, dry the tire and lift the tape for about two inches in each direction from the mark, exposing the stitching. Cut each of the stitches very carefully along the distance of the lifted tape. You'll see another tape on the inside, and you may have to cut stitches on this tape, too, but only on one side. Once enough of the tape is unstitched, lift the tube out. Then inflate the tire just enough to locate the puncture. Listen for the hiss of the leaking air, and you can usually locate the hole by sound.

If it is a small leak, place just the tube in some water and watch for the telltale bubbles. After you find the puncture, dry and clean the tube, then apply some rubber cement. While waiting for the cement to dry, select a patch that will adequately cover the hole. If one is not ready-cut, you will have to cut one from the larger sheet included in most patch kits. When the rubber cement has dried, peel off the protective covering on the patch, trying not to handle the sticky side, and apply the patch to the tube.

Before tucking the tube back into the casing, locate the puncture in the casing to see whether the glass or whatever else caused it is still imbedded in the tire. If it is, remove it very carefully. Don't lose it in the tire, or you'll end up with another puncture.

Should there be a hole large enough to allow the tube to protrude, or if the casing is weak, cut a small patch from the sidewall of the piece of spare silk casing material mentioned earlier and attach it on the inside of the punctured casing. Clean the area around the hole and apply some rubber cement. Allow it to dry and then apply the patch. After this, sprinkle some talcum powder around the patched area to prevent the cemented area from sticking.

We normally leave the inner tape unstitched simply because there's no practical way to sew it up without risking puncturing the tube with the needle. Just carefully tuck it back in the tire, making sure that it lies flat without any wrinkles or folds.

To resew the cord properly, use the original holes from the factory stitching. Start a few stitches before the cut ones to ensure a secure overlap between the old and new. After you've

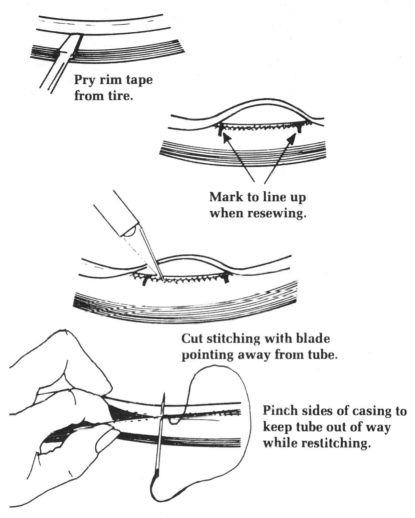

Pry rim tape from tire.

Mark to line up when resewing.

Cut stitching with blade pointing away from tube.

Pinch sides of casing to keep tube out of way while restitching.

Illustration 3–1. Crucial steps in tubular tire repair.

finished sewing in one direction, go back in the other direction but change the stitching so a cross-stitch results. Then spread some rubber cement on the stitched seam and on the seam tape. Allow it to dry, and glue the tape back on, making sure the pen mark matches up.

Unless the puncture was very minor, it's advisable to use a repaired tubular only for training or spares. For racing or touring, it is best to start with undamaged tires.

Replacing a Broken Spoke

Sooner or later you'll be out riding, and mixed in with the sounds of a country road you'll hear the unmistakable sound of a spoke breaking. Don't feel bad, spokes break for even the best of riders, and mechanics.

When you break a spoke, you are faced with a decision, should you replace it on the road or try to make it home for repairs. This question is normally answered by whether you have a replacement spoke and tools with you or not. If not, cut or break the broken spoke off and head for home, pedaling as easy as you can. Once a spoke is gone, the wheel loses a lot of strength, and without much force, other spokes will soon break.

The first step in repairing a broken spoke is to remove the wheel from the bike and take it with you to buy replacement spokes. Ideally you should do this before your spoke ever breaks so you have spares always on hand. Also, get a spoke wrench and a freewheel remover for your particular wheel.

Next, remove the tire and tube from the wheel and clean off any excess grease or adhesive. If it is a rear wheel and the broken spoke is on the cluster side, you must remove the gear cluster and spoke protector. This requires a freewheel remover. With the cluster and guard removed, you are ready to replace the spoke.

By looking at the hub, you can quickly see which way to put in your new spoke. For those who haven't seen spokes close-up before, they are threaded on one end and bent like a fishhook (with a flange instead of a point) on the other end. The flanged end goes into the hub, and the threaded end goes into the rim. A threaded nipple goes through the rim and screws onto the spoke, fastening the spoke to the rim. By adjusting tension on the different spokes, you can pull a wheel into perfect trueness and roundness.

To put in a spoke, slip the threaded end through the hole in the hub and pull the spoke into the wheel until the flange meets the hub. At this time, the spoke will not be at its final destination at the hole in the rim, but don't worry. You still have to weave the new spoke through the old ones to get it where it goes.

Photograph 3–4. Be sure you weave the new spoke over and under the other spokes correctly.

Be careful that you have your spoke woven correctly over and under the other spokes. Spokes alternate in their direction from the hub, going in opposite ways. From the hole in the hub where you are going to replace the spoke, skip one spoke and trace the pattern of the next spoke; it will go the way you want the replacement to go. On a three-cross wheel, a wheel where each spoke crosses three other spokes on its way to the rim, the first two spokes are usually crossed on the same side, and the third spoke is crossed on the opposite side.

When moving the spoke, it's all right to slightly bend it, as you'll straighten it when tightening. Once the threaded end is through the hole in the rim, recheck its weaving and thread the nipple on until it is snug. Once the nipple is snug, use your spoke wrench to tighten it to about the same tension as the other spokes. By alternately squeezing the new spoke and an old one with your hand, you should be able to get a feel for how much tension to use.

If you are only replacing one spoke, or the wheel isn't too far out of balance, you won't need a truing stand. If you are making an emergency repair on the road, put the wheel on the bike and use the brake calipers as a truing guide. For on-the-road repairs, this completes the job. Put on the tire, remount the wheel, and you are off and riding. However, when you get home you should retrue the wheel.

Truing the Wheel

Truing a wheel means getting it as close to perfectly round as you can. To true a wheel, place the wheel in a truing stand and adjust the calipers until they lightly touch the outermost part of the rim when the wheel turns. From this point on, remember that in all operations with your spokes you must do everything in pairs.

When truing a wheel, you have to realize that if you tighten a spoke that started at the left flange of the hub, you have to loosen one next to it that started from the right flange. This will keep the wheel "in round." It doesn't matter what side of the spoke you start with as long as you loosen an opposite one. You should never take more than a half-turn at a time with the spoke wrench. Take a half-turn on each pair of spokes in the trouble area and give the wheel a spin to check it before taking another half-turn.

If the wheel is touching the right side of the truing stand (all directions are from a head-on view), you will want to tighten spokes that originate on the left side of the hub. Normally it will take four spokes to pull a minor variation into line. That means you will tighten two spokes and loosen two spokes. If any part of the wheel does not touch the caliper set to within ⅛ inch of the wheel, you have finished this part of the truing procedure.

Next you must check to be sure your wheel is round. Move the calipers up higher onto the wheel until the outer two edges of the rim almost touch the bottom of the caliper arm of the truing stand. Spin the wheel slowly to see if any parts of the wheel touch the stand before others. If any parts touch, tighten the spokes in that area to pull that part of the rim up. Remember to always tighten pairs of spokes, one that originates on the right of the hub and one that originates on the left of the hub. This will prevent you from pulling the wheel out of true while you round it. If one part of the rim is too high, loosen a pair of

Photograph 3–5. A truing stand such as the one pictured here is equipped with calipers that allow a wheel to be adjusted to very close tolerances.

spokes. Once you have it in round, go back and check the trueness and make necessary adjustments.

When track racers build a wheel, they alternate from checking roundness to trueness until they have no more than a hair's difference in any dimension. For street riding, get as close as you can. Take the wheel off the stand and put it on the floor and apply your body weight to it about every ten inches around the circumference of the wheel to "spring" the wheel. This will give you a good idea of how the wheel will ride after a few miles. Now, put it back on the stand and check for trueness and roundness. If both are satisfactory, reassemble the wheel and you are done. If not, continue to adjust.

Why Do Spokes Break?

Spokes fail for a variety of reasons.

Overstressed spokes: The wheel isn't properly built, so certain spokes are overstressed. This is where the beginner gets into trouble with a spoke wrench.

Light spokes: The spokes are too light for the service. If you weigh 200 pounds or you carry touring loads, don't try to use 15- or 16-gauge, double-butted spokes. If you find your freewheel-side spokes breaking regularly, settle for plain 14-gauge spokes and accept the tiny weight penalty.

Defective spokes: This seems to be a problem with the cheapest spokes and with expensive, stainless steel spokes.

Wheel construction: The wheel construction is wrong for the service. This is less important than the above reasons. Four-cross, low-flange wheels are less prone to spoke failure than the more normal three-cross, high-flange construction.

Freewheel Removal and Installation

Replacing broken spokes and changing your gearing arrangement are the two most common reasons why you may need to remove the freewheel from your bicycle. Whatever the reason, one thing is certain: without the proper tools, freewheel removal is impossible.

Actually, there are two different aspects to freewheel removal: removal of the entire freewheel assembly from the hub and removal of the sprockets, or cogs, from the freewheel body. First, we'll look at removal of the entire freewheel; later, we'll deal with getting individual sprockets off of a freewheel body.

With the exception of the Regina Futura, the Maillard Helicomatic, and the Shimano Freehub systems (more on them in a moment), you must have a freewheel removal tool to separate a freewheel from the hub it's mounted on. The removal tool is nothing more than a cylindrical socket with splines or prongs on one end, which fit into the freewheel body, and large flats on the other end, which you grasp with a large wrench or bench vise.

Although all freewheels have either grooves or notches to receive the removal tool's splines or prongs, the dimensions of these splines and notches are not standardized from brand to brand. Thus, it is vitally important that you know what type of freewheel you are working on and use the proper removal tool

Photograph 3–6. Freewheel removal tools. It is vitally important to use the tool that fits your freewheel.

to get it off. Close fits are never close enough; in fact, they're usually disastrous. Stripped splines and irrevocably damaged freewheel bodies are common casualties of the "close enough" school of freewheel removal. Moreover, if you do strip the splines or notches out of a freewheel body, the chances are excellent that you'll never get the freewheel off the hub.

How to Use a Removal Tool

To remove a standard freewheel, you will need the correct removal tool and a bench vise or, in lieu of that, an extra-large (12-inch minimum) adjustable wrench of the type made by Crescent.

The first order of business is to remove the hub's quick-release assembly. Install the removal tool into the freewheel splines or notches, then replace the quick-release assembly. Thread on the quick-release so that it holds the removal tool firmly in place. This simple trick will prevent the tool from slipping out of place and damaging the splines or notches. If the hub does not have a quick-release, unscrew the axle nut, install the removal tool, then reinstall the axle nut and snug it down to retain the tool. If you have an older Regina or Atom removal tool, you will find that you need to remove the hub locknuts to install the tool.

Freewheels attach tightly to their hubs, and the fine pitch of their threads only encourages this bond. Thus, to remove a freewheel, you must apply a significant amount of leverage. The best lever is the wheel itself—almost 14 inches worth. Simply slip the flats of the freewheel tool between the jaws of a bench vise and turn the wheel counterclockwise.

If you do not have a bench vise, you will need a large adjustable wrench to provide enough leverage. You can wrestle with the wheel in whatever manner you like, but here's the method that works best for us. Stand the wheel up on end, parallel to your body and with the freewheel opposite you. Hold the top of the wheel with your left hand. Reach over the wheel with your right hand and grasp the end of the wrench handle (choking up reduces your leverage). Now take a deep breath and push down with all your might. Presto. As soon as the

Photograph 3–7. If a bench vise is not available, substitute a large adjustable wrench. Use your axle nut or quick-release assembly to hold the removal tool in place while applying leverage.

freewheel breaks free, stop. Remove the axle quick-release or axle nuts. Then unscrew the freewheel the rest of the way.

Not every freewheel removal operation is this easy, of course. If the freewheel is especially stubborn, drip penetrating lubricant into the mounting threads. Be sure to allow the lubricant time to work. Tapping lightly on the freewheel body may also help to unstick it.

In extreme cases, you may have to apply heat to expand the freewheel away from the hub. Use a propane torch with a low, feathery flame and touch it to the freewheel body as sparingly as possible. Work carefully and check the freewheel often to see if it is loose. Heat generally takes the temper out of the freewheel body. Discard a freewheel that has been removed by this method since the long-term integrity of the body is dubious at best. Also, be sure to repack the hub bearings with fresh grease if heat has been used.

Incidentally, the leverage necessary to remove a freewheel points to an obvious rule: never install a freewheel on an unspoked hub. Similarly, never unspoke a wheel without removing the freewheel first. You will find it virtually impossible to remove a conventional freewheel from a bare hub.

Freewheel Installation

Freewheel installation is straightforward; you just screw the freewheel back onto the hub. First, as with any threaded fastener, clean threads are essential. Be sure to spiff up the threads inside the freewheel, as well as the ones on the hub. An old toothbrush and a pan of solvent, such as kerosene, are the tools of choice here.

Second, do not forget the Mechanics' First Commandment: Always Grease Threads. If you neglect to grease the freewheel body threads before you install it, you deserve whatever agonies you encounter next time you have to remove the thing.

Third, freewheel threads are of a fairly fine pitch; moreover, the threads on the hub are rolled from relatively soft aluminum material. These two factors mean that cross-threading is a very real possibility and a disastrously expensive one, should it occur. To avoid cross-threading, place the freewheel body flat against the hub threads. Unscrew the freewheel until you feel the first thread drop into place. Then carefully thread on the freewheel. If you encounter resistance, stop and check your work. Once you have the first three threads engaged, you can proceed more or less fearlessly; you've probably got it on right.

Finally, it's unnecessary to use the freewheel tool to tighten the body onto the hub. It will become sufficiently tight as you ride.

Futuras and Helicomatics

The Regina Futura and the Maillard Helicomatic are relatively recent designs that do not employ standard freewheel attachment methods. The Regina is the more unusual of the two designs and allows the fastest sprocket changing in town. The Futura sprockets are not separate pieces but parts of an unchangeable block. The block engages the freewheel body/hub unit with a bayonet mount. Push and turn, the block comes off. Push and turn, it's back in place.

The Helicomatic hub/freewheel system also gathers the sprockets into a modular block. The block is retained by a simple lockring. Unscrew the lockring, and the entire sprocket block unwinds off its helix. Maillard lockring wrenches should be available from any bicycle shop that carries Peugeot, Motobecane, or Trek bicycles. In an emergency, you can unscrew the lockring with a pair of locking pliers; doing so, however, may damage the lockring serrations, making future use of the proper tool more difficult. Incidentally, it is not necessary to remove the sprocket block from the hub to change individual sprockets in this system. They can be changed using chain whips in the conventional manner described below. The two top sprockets thread on, and the rest of the sprockets are located by splines.

Shimano Freehub

The Shimano Freehub is an in-between design, neither as revolutionary as the Regina nor as conventional as a standard freewheel system. As the name implies, the freewheel mechanism and the hub are integrated into a single unit. Thus, the freewheel does not come off in the usual manner. Rather, the sprockets are removable from the Freehub, leaving the freewheel mechanism intact. Sprocket removal on the Freehub is accomplished with chain whips. The smallest sprocket unscrews. All the other sprockets are splined and will slip off once the first sprocket is removed.

On most models, the Freehub mechanism itself can be removed from the hub, if necessary. This procedure requires special Shimano tools, which should be available from your dealer. Follow the instructions that come with the tools.

Sprocket Removal

Sprocket removal is accomplished with a tool called a chain whip, which is nothing more than a lever with a length of chain attached to it. The chain wraps around the freewheel sprocket, providing a means by which to unscrew it.

Almost every freewheel in the world is assembled in the same manner: the smallest sprocket threads onto the body and serves to retain the rest of the sprockets, which are either splined

Photograph 3—8. Install the chain whips on the sprockets so that their handles criss-cross. Squeeze the handles together to unscrew the outer sprocket.

onto the body or threaded onto it. We have already described some exceptions to this design. Here, we're concerned with how to remove standard sprockets from a freewheel body.

Chain whips are best bought in pairs because having two of these handy devices means that you can change most sprockets without removing the freewheel from the hub. Sprocket removal is effortless. Simply wrap one whip clockwise around the sprocket you wish to unscrew. The face of the tool should be against the sprocket. Now wrap the other tool counterclockwise around a sprocket two or more positions away from the sprocket you're unscrewing. Again, the angled face of the tool

Photograph 3–9. To unscrew a cog using a single chain whip, immobilize the freewheel body with a freewheel vise secured in the jaws of a bench vise.

should be against the sprocket. Install the tools so that the handles criss-cross. Squeeze the handles of the tools together; the outer sprocket will unscrew.

If you have but one chain whip, you can still unscrew the freewheel sprockets, but you must have some method of immobilizing the freewheel body. Generally, the procedure is to unscrew the freewheel from the hub, then use a freewheel vise to hold the assembly stationary while you unscrew the cog. This is a satisfactory system if you own a bench vise by which to grip the freewheel vise and a freewheel removal tool to remove the freewheel.

Certain freewheels with no splined sprockets must be disassembled this way. To remove the largest two sprockets on an all-threaded freewheel, you place the small sprocket in the freewheel vise, then use the chain whip to unscrew the largest sprockets. There is, of course, one more complication to remember: the top (largest) two sprockets have left-hand threads, so you must remember to unscrew them the opposite way you unscrew all the other sprockets, and screw them on backwards, too.

Sprocket Replacement

Freewheel sprockets go back on in the reverse order of how they come off, but note these two similarities with the installation of freewheels on hubs. First, it is unnecessary to use the chain whips to tighten the sprockets onto the body; leg power will wrench them on tightly enough. Second, don't forget the Mechanics' First Commandment: Always Grease Threads. To assemble a freewheel without first greasing the threads of the sprockets and the body is to ensure a sweaty, curse-filled afternoon sometime in the future, as you struggle to divorce two happily married metal components.

Part Four
Drivetrain and Brake Repairs

Adjusting Your Brakes

It's hard to name a bicycle component more important than the brakes. Yet, as any bicycle repairman can attest, most cyclists keep their brakes in minimal repair. How about you? Are your brakes adjusted well enough to get you out of any jam you might pedal into? If not, an hour of your time and possibly a few dollars can put your brakes in top condition.

Several problems befall brakes. You may find yourself fixing any or all of the following.

Excess friction in the moving parts (hand lever, cable and casing, brake arm pivot points) robs energy from the assigned task of slowing the bicycle down. The friction also fools you into thinking you really are braking hard because you're squeezing so hard at a time when you aren't.

Misaligned brake shoes work poorly because the rubber pads don't strike the rim squarely. This can lead to flat tires from sidewall abrasion, rapid and uneven wear of your brake pads, and inferior braking performance. Or your brake pads may be so badly worn, especially if they're worn unevenly, that they need replacement.

If the brake mechanism isn't centered over the wheel, one brake shoe may drag on the rim constantly. While it's possible for this to be a mere annoyance in otherwise well-adjusted brakes, it feels awful, and it introduces a constant drag that obscures the nice road feel you should get in your fingertips when you apply your brakes.

Your brakes may be too loose so that you have to squeeze the hand lever almost to the end of its range of motion just to get the brake pads to touch the rim. Unduly loose brakes don't give you enough stopping power. Most well-designed brake sets (including some of the very cheapest ones sold) can be adjusted to offer so much stopping power that you'll be squeezing as hard as you can (and locking your wheels) before you run out of lever travel. Your bike should be in such condition.

Brakes may also be too tight so they rub the rim constantly, creating constant drag on the bike and needless wear on the brakes. Or perhaps a warped or dented rim strikes the brake pads as it revolves between them.

Brakes may be mounted loosely on the bicycle frame. This introduces wobble and clatter into the brake system and also increases the chances of a serious accident from a brake coming off the frame and tangling in the spokes.

Overhauling Your Brakes

Begin your overhaul by making sure your brakes can't come off the frame. Is the nut that holds them onto the frame loose? Or once you've loosened it, does it spin freely? If it does, it might vibrate right off someday and cause you to crash. Some brakes have a small rubber ring embedded in the mounting nut. The rubber ring keeps the nut from spinning freely and ensures that the nut won't vibrate off.

If your brakes don't have this rubber insert, invest a dollar in a tiny bottle of any brand of anaerobic adhesive. (Anaerobic adhesive gums up the threads so the nut comes loose only when you want it to.) You may want to put it on other bicycle parts as well, but don't get it near any moving parts, and don't use very much. A little goes a long way.

Now look over your rims. They're part of your braking system, and you can't do an overhaul without checking them, too. Lift the bicycle so one wheel is a few inches off the floor and give the wheel a spin. Does it wobble from side to side because of a potato-chip-shaped warp? Use a spoke wrench to fix the warp, or if you prefer, have a shop true your wheels for you, but don't neglect this part of the adjustment.

The biggest portion of the job of overhauling your brakes will probably be eliminating unnecessary friction from the moving parts. Start by loosening the cable inner wire from the brake's binder bolt so you can free the cable from the hand lever. Does the hand lever swing freely when the cable isn't attached? If it doesn't, squirt some oil at the hand lever pivot points. Swing the lever several times. If the lever still doesn't swing freely, gently bend it to one side and, while continuing to bend, swing it up and down a few times. Then bend it to the other side and repeat.

While you're working on your hand levers, make sure they're securely attached to the handlebars. If they need tightening, give a firm twist to the mounting screw (usually found in the throat of the lever housing).

Your next target is cable friction, an especially common cause of brake malfunctions. There are two potential problems here: excessive cable casing length and poor lubrication.

Cable casing length is an often ignored but significant source of brake system friction. Your cable casings should be no longer than necessary to reach from the brake lever to their endpoint (either the front brake or the frame's top tube) in a smooth but tight arc. Any extra casing length adds a lot of friction. If you glance at any photograph of bicycle racers, you'll see they're all outfitted with very short brake cable casings.

Odds are your bicycle came from the factory with cable casings a few inches too long. To see how much casing length you can do without, remove the inner wire and hold the casing in its normal position on the bicycle. Move the casing to describe a tight arc between its endpoints and cut off the surplus with sharp wire cutters (small wire cutters will do the job if they're sharp). Don't forget the little bit of cable that reaches up off the top tube and down to the rear brake. Bicycles are often sold with this little loop describing a double-S curve. By shortening this little bit of cable, you can eliminate a lot of friction.

Now grease your inner wire. Work as much grease as you possibly can into the space between the inner wire and the casing. It's important that the cable innards stay well greased otherwise moisture will cause those innards to rust and stick to one another.

Finally, see if your brake arms pivot freely. If they can't, try lightly loosening their mounting bolts. Those bolts should be just loose enough for the brake to function freely—and not loose enough to allow the brake arms to slope sideways.

Photograph 4–1. Shorten excessively long cable casings to reduce friction. Use a swift, firm grip and a sharp pair of wire cutters to ensure a clean cut.

Brake Pads

Inspect your brake shoes and rubber pads. If they're worn unevenly, replace them. If they're mounted so they don't contact the rim squarely, loosen the mounting nut and reposition them.

Make sure you tighten the mounting nut securely, but don't overdo it—you can easily snap the nut off. This mounting nut is another good place for a drop of anaerobic adhesive. And if your brakes have been squealing, gently bend the arms so the fronts of the brake pads contact the rim slightly ahead of the rear.

A lot of people resign themselves to having one brake shoe drag on the rim. They shouldn't. Sidepull brakes can be centered in less than a minute once you learn the trick. For most brands of sidepull brakes, you'll need a special centering tool—an extra-thin, ten-millimeter wrench. If you're lucky, you may find one at your local bike shop. If not, you can devise your own by buying a regular wrench at the hardware store and taking it down on a grinding wheel. You will also need a regular ten-millimeter wrench.

Put the regular ten-millimeter wrench on the cap nut (also called the acorn adjusting nut) that holds the whole brake assembly onto the pivot bolt. Now put your extra-thin, ten-millimeter wrench on the locknut that sits right behind the cap nut. Tighten the two nuts against one another. Now leave one of the two wrenches on its nut and move the other wrench to the brake mounting nut that holds the whole brake on the frame. Now, by turning both wrenches in unison, you can rotate the brake pivot bolt—and along with it the spring that centers the calipers and brake shoes. With the slightest twist of your wrist, the brake will be perfectly centered over the wheel.

If your bicycle has the new sidepull brakes without a cap nut, the job is even easier. You won't have to hunt for any extra-thin wrenches. The head of the pivot bolt is broached for a six-millimeter Allen wrench. Insert the Allen wrench there. Put a ten-millimeter wrench on the mounting nut in the rear and rotate it.

If your bicycle has centerpull brakes, the job is no more difficult. You may be able to center the brake with your bare hands. See if you can rotate the bridge (the piece of metal in which the caliper pivots and springs are located) by hand. If you can, that's not necessarily a sign that the brake is dangerously loose, but make sure the mounting nut can't vibrate off. If you can't budge the bridge by hand, use a large metal-eating tool, preferably a set of arc-joint pliers. Slightly loosen the ten-

Photograph 4–2. To center sidepull brakes, first tighten the cap nut against the locknut. Then move one wrench to the rear mounting nut and move both wrenches in unison to rotate the entire assembly.

millimeter mounting nut, use the tool to rotate the bridge, and hold the bridge in position as you retighten the nut.

Tightening Brake Cables

Tightening brake cables is a job that drives many home mechanics to distraction. You have to squeeze the brake shoes shut, pull the cable inner wire taut, and tighten the binder bolt all at once. No wonder various companies manufacture a tool called a third hand and another tool called a fourth hand. But you and I can do a fine job with just two hands and a little ingenuity. The procedure is the same for both centerpull and sidepull brakes.

Photograph 4–3. Wind the cable around your needle-nose pliers until your brakes are a bit on the tight side, then tighten the binder bolt.

To restore your brakes to working order after removing them, first rethread the cable through the loosened binder bolt. Now take a pair of needle-nose pliers and grip the cable just underneath the binder bolt. Rotate the pliers while keeping a tight grip on the cable. You'll wind the cable around your pliers as you would wind spaghetti around a fork. This automatically shuts the brake shoes.

Wind cable until the brakes are as tight as you want them (you want them on the tight side to allow for cable stretch). Now, while keeping the cable wound up, use your other hand (and for most brands, a nine-millimeter wrench) to tighten the binder bolt. When the bolt is snug enough to keep the cable from slipping, set your needle-nose pliers down and carefully tighten the cable binder bolt the rest of the way.

For sidepull brakes, a good rule of thumb is to tighten the binder bolt as much as you can with one finger on the wrench. It's easy to strip the threads and snap the bolt off if you use your whole hand. And look at where the cable passes through the hole in the binder bolt. When it looks substantially crimped, you've tightened it enough to keep it from slipping.

For centerpull brakes, you'll need to finish tightening the binder bolt with two wrenches since the bolt is part of that little, free-floating cable yoke. Hold the binder bolt's rear end steady with one wrench and tighten the nut onto the cable with the other wrench. Your binder bolt is just as delicate as the one on a sidepull brake so don't use all your might.

If you have trouble tightening your cable this way, a third hand tool (available at most bike shops) will hold the brake shoes shut for you. By the way, a small C-clamp makes a very serviceable third hand tool.

Now that you've finished your overhaul, be prudent and keep your brakes in good condition. They'll return the favor.

Troubleshooting and Adjusting Gears

Pity the poor derailleur. Whenever a bicycle doesn't shift well, people assume it's the derailleur's fault. The blame is often misplaced.

True, the derailleur is the kingpin of the bicycle's intricate shifting mechanism, but it works in close contact with many other components: the chain, chainwheels, and the freewheel cogs. Any of these, especially when coated with dirt, can cause poor shifting, scraping, grinding, and other drivetrain problems. In this chapter, we'll examine the drivetrain and fix these problems one by one.

Cleanliness Solves Many Problems

It's no fun cleaning greasy dirt out of your drivetrain, but it's the best way to start an attack on drivetrain problems. Dirt sneaks into bearing surfaces and other nooks and crannies so parts that should move freely get gummed up. Cleaning out this dirt will magically cure some problems, and it will make the solutions to others more obvious.

Chain

We'll begin with the chain, partly because it's simple and partly because a freshly cleaned and oiled chain works noticeably better than a dirty one.

Chains won't last forever, and you should expect to replace yours every couple of years, especially if you ride a lot or let the chain get rusty. When the chain wears out, the link pins chew at (and enlarge) the holes in the chain's inner sideplates, giving the chain too much flex in all directions. Not only does this make for more reluctant shifting (because the chain has a tendency to flex sideways as it spans the gap between the derailleur and the cog), but also each chain link becomes slightly longer. As a result, the chain no longer meshes with the cogs and chainwheel teeth and grinds them. It also tends to skip up over the teeth of the smallest rear cog when you pedal hard.

To check for chain wear, reach for a section of chain wrapped around a front chainwheel. Using thumb and forefinger, try to pick a single chain link up off the chainwheel teeth. It shouldn't move more than ⅛ inch. If it can be moved more than that, there is too much flex in the link pins, and it's a sign that the chain should be replaced.

A more elaborate and accurate way of measuring chain wear is to take the chain off the bike as described below and stretch it out on a flat surface. Measure the length of a 24-link section. A new chain will measure 12 inches. When a chain measures more than 12⅛ inches, the chain is worn out.

If your chain looks dirty, it is, and it should be taken off the bike and cleaned. A 10-speed chain has no master link; you remove the chain from the bike by cutting it with a chain-link tool. Set the chain in the tool and screw in the chain-tool punch. The punch will push a chain-link pin out of the link. When the pin is almost clear of the chain's inner plates, unscrew the chain-tool punch. You should be able to pull the link apart now. To replace the chain later on, you'll use the same chain-tool punch to push the link pin back where it belongs; then you'll put the link in the chain tool's other notch and screw in the punch to

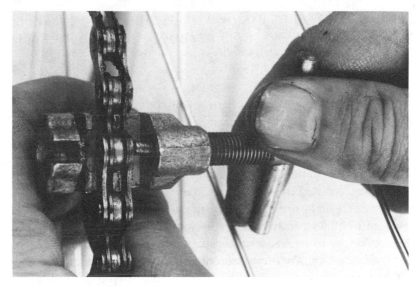

Photograph 4–4. To remove the chain from a 10 speed bike, cut it with a chain-link tool.

flex the link sideways, restoring the link's flexibility.

Soak the chain in a can of kerosene and clean off any dirt with an old paintbrush or rag. Let the chain dry. When you put it back on the bike, give each link a drop of light oil. Allow the oil to penetrate the links and wipe off the outer plates with a rag; oil on the outside surfaces of a chain only attracts more dirt.

Freewheel

Now remove the rear wheel from the bicycle so you can have a closer look at your next target—the freewheel. Is it dirty? Clean away the caked dirt with a screwdriver and finish the job with a rag soaked in kerosene. If the freewheel is exceptionally dirty, remove it from the hub with a freewheel remover and soak it in kerosene. Then let it dry thoroughly so the kerosene has a chance to drain out of the bearings. Whether you soak the freewheel or not, squirt light oil into the gap between the small cog and the freewheel body to lubricate the bearings. Spin the freewheel so the oil is well distributed among the bearings, and use a rag to clean up the excess that leaks back out.

If the teeth on your freewheel cogs have rounded corners from the chain grating on them, this may be a cause of drivetrain problems, such as the chain skipping on the smallest cog.

Rear Derailleur

We're finally ready to examine your rear derailleur. Start this task with the rear wheel off the bike so you can more easily manipulate the derailleur mechanism. The derailleur has two spring-loaded pivots: one takes up chain slack by rotating the chain cage toward the rear of the bike, and the other pulls the chain cage out (except when you shift into a lower gear). A few rear derailleurs have a third spring-loaded pivot, which pulls the entire derailleur body toward the rear of the bike.

Get your hands dirty and flex the derailleur along these spring-loaded pivots. When you let go, the spring should snap the derailleur back to its original position. If it doesn't, clean the dirt out and lubricate the mechanism with light oil. Whether you clean the derailleur with a rag or use the immersion method depends on the amount of dirt present. Make sure you thoroughly clean and lubricate the two rollers in the chain cage.

Now that you've cleaned your derailleur so that it pivots freely, you're almost finished. The only procedures left are to clean and grease the derailleur cable (if necessary); adjust the range-of-motion limiting screws; and on a few models, adjust the angle at which the derailleur body rests. Overhauling the cable is a simple operation, but the other two tasks may need some explanation.

With the rear wheel back on the bicycle, shift to your highest and lowest gears and observe how wide a range of motion the derailleur has. It should reach just far enough in each direction to sit directly underneath the cogs on either end of the freewheel. If the range of motion needs to be altered, first make sure the problem is not caused by a cable that is too tight or too loose. Then turn the high- and low-gear adjusting screws found on all rear derailleurs as needed to properly establish the limits for the unit's movement.

The last step is only necessary for a few rear derailleurs—the resting angle adjustment. This is best left alone, especially if there's no apparent need to change it. But if the chain sometimes skips over the smallest cog, try turning this adjusting screw counterclockwise, to position the derailleur farther forward and wrap more chain around the cogs. However, don't change the resting angle so much that the jockey roller collides with the largest cog when you shift into low gear.

Front Derailleur

Does your front derailleur obey your wishes? Or does it throw the chain nowhere in particular, make awful noises that you can't get rid of, and respond begrudgingly to your tugging at the shift lever? And does the chain have a mind of its own? Problems of this type can all be solved with a methodical overhaul of the front end of your drivetrain.

Earlier we called for a little loving care, some kerosene, and a lot of old rags to make the rear end of the drivetrain (freewheel, rear derailleur, and chain) work better. Overhauling the front end of the drivetrain is a different sort of job for a few reasons.

To begin with, the front shift is inherently a cruder mechanism. The front derailleur can give only a sideways shove to a chain under tension, whereas the rear derailleur cradles and guides the slack side of the chain.

Manufacturers of moderately priced bicycles have traditionally built the front end of the drivetrain to more casual manufacturing tolerances than the rear end, and it's quite possible that you can improve your drivetrain's front-end performance with some well-planned grinding and bending. Fortunately, newer bicycle models need much less of this sort of retrofitting than bikes from the early 1970s and before. And cotterless cranksets are exempt from all bending and grinding.

Before you do anything drastic, get out your tools, rags, and kerosene and see how much you can improve shifting performance through cleanliness. Lift the chain off the chainwheels and around the outside of the large chainwheel. Tuck it back around the rear of the chainwheels, and it will dangle from the rear of the front derailleur as if the chain weren't there.

You want to see how easily the front derailleur pivots through its range of motion. Most modern front derailleurs swing the chain cage upward as they swing it outward. Some older designs use a push-rod mechanism, which moves the chain cage sideways.

Whichever kind of front derailleur you have, you want it to operate without signs of stickiness. Grab it and manipulate it through its range of motion. It should move smoothly, and the return spring should snap it back to rest position when you let go. If it doesn't, disassemble the mechanism, clean it, grease the bearing surfaces, and reassemble. If the derailleur cable passes through a short casing, grease that portion of the cable. If the cable goes around a steel turnaround fitting, grease the point of contact with the fitting.

See that the derailleur is mounted as low as possible on the frame's seat tube. It should clear the large chainwheel by only a few millimeters. The chain cage's sideplates should be parallel to the chain. If they are not parallel, rotate the derailleur on the seat tube until they are.

Photograph 4–5. Shifting performance can be improved by giving the front derailleur cage a slightly narrower nose.

If necessary, adjust the range-of-motion limiting screws to the following specifications. When the chain is on the small front chainwheel and largest rear cog (L-1), the derailleur chain cage's inner plate should not scrape the chain. The derailleur should have enough, but just barely enough, range of motion to meet these requirements.

If you've done all the above and your drivetrain still misbehaves, scrub down for bicycle surgery. You're about to improve on the manufacturer's efforts.

The first step is to check the shape of the front derailleur chain cage. Most manufacturers will have bent the front of each plate slightly toward the other. By giving the chain cage a narrower nose in this manner, shifting performance is improved. The narrow nose derails the chain with greater authority than a lateral shove from the sideplate.

If your derailleur cage is not bent in this way, take your pliers and gently bend the front of the outside plate about 2 millimeters inward. Bend the inside plate the same distance toward the outer plate. Check to see if the derailleur now shifts the way you want. If it does not, continue to try minor adjustments to the nose of the plates until you get it the way you want it. The precise adjustment needed will depend a lot on the differential between your chainwheels and the quality of your chain. If your bike has a cotterless crankset, you should be finished now. Cottered crank people should read on.

Lateral Misplacement

This increases lateral chain deflection, and that makes the drivetrain run and shift poorly. Cottered cranks are built with a great deal of play in their design. The collar-receiving flat spot on the crank axle is about ¼ inch wider than the cotter pin. This allows you to move the chainwheels ¼ inch laterally whenever you remove the cotter pin.

Check the lateral placement (more commonly known as chain line alignment) by putting the bike in L-1 gear and standing behind the rear wheel. Close one eye and look down the drivetrain. The middle cog on the freewheel should line up with the space between the two chainwheels. If it doesn't, you may want to remove the cotter pin, slide the chainwheels sideways, and reinstall the cotter pin. If this is a new task for you, read the chapter on cottered cranks found earlier in this book before you jump into it. You may damage the crank bearings if you don't follow the proper procedure.

Now, with your chainwheels in proper chain line alignment, see whether they're too close together. Put the bike in L-5 gear (small chainwheel, smallest cog). The chain should not scrape against the inside of the large chainwheel. If it does, you should bend the large chainwheel slightly outward. The best way to do this is with a special chainwheel bending tool, but you can find plenty of usable substitutes in your home toolbox.

Among the candidates for ad hoc chainwheel bending tools are the claw end of a carpenter's hammer, a hefty screwdriver, the part of an adjustable hacksaw frame that ordinarily holds the far end of the hacksaw blade, and any other thin piece of metal strong enough to withstand some sideways bending. Slide your piece of metal between the two chainwheels so one end rests near one of the fixing bolts (the bolts that attach the chainwheels to one another). Bend outward. Do the same for each of the fixing bolts.

Another good bending technique is to use arc-joint pliers. Grip the large chainwheel as close to its center as you can and bend it from several points around the circumference. If all this bending causes interference problems with one of those pie plate chainguards, we suggest removing it. Rubber bands around the pants cuffs cause less trouble.

Now after all this work, do you still have a drivetrain problem? One common mishap occurs like this: you're riding along in L-1 gear and the chain spontaneously derails to the inside. Or you're riding in H-1 (large chainwheel, largest rear cog) and the same thing happens. Many mechanics try to "fix" the L-1 derailment by adjusting the front derailleur so it constantly pushes the chain toward the chainwheel. That's incorrect. The derailleur should touch the chain only during shifting.

These derailments occur because the chainwheel teeth are too blunt due to lax quality control and ill-placed lumps of chrome plating. Top-quality chainwheels have sharp teeth with carefully designed and machined profiles. The chain walks up off the top of blunt teeth, but it stays engaged on sharp teeth.

To make your chainwheels shift like good ones, hold a file against the side of the teeth. Rotate the cranks and gently grind some metal away. You don't need to do much grinding; a minute or two should be plenty. Don't worry about the ill effects of removing the chrome plating. Oil from your chain will keep the chainwheels from rusting.

Cleanliness is 90 percent of all maintenance required to keep your drivetrain rolling. A thorough cleaning, coupled with proper lubrication and adjustment, will make any gearing system, no matter how cheap or expensive, work quite well.

Fitting and Repairing Cables

Think of your bike's cables as its central nervous system. Cables carry your messages to the vital parts, telling them how and when you want them to move. Thus, cables are an extremely important part of your bicycle, which from time to time will need some repair.

The preceding two chapters provide general advice on how to clean and adjust your bike's gear and brake assemblies. This final chapter uses a series of drawings to illustrate information concerning the selection, installation, repair, and maintenance of cables.

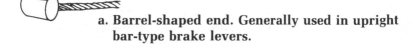

a. Barrel-shaped end. Generally used in upright bar-type brake levers.

b. Mushroom-shaped end. Used in hooded levers and upright bar types.

c. Open cable end.

Illustration 4–1. The most frequently encountered types of cable ends.

Illustration 4–1 shows the most frequently encountered types of cable ends. The most common cables sold have a barrel shape at one end and a mushroom at the other so they will fit different types of levers. You just snip off the end you don't need when installing the cable. More expensive cables made by the top component manufacturers have only one fitting as needed for a particular model lever. These cables are heavier, containing more strands of wire than the cheaper ones, and are sometimes prestretched by the manufacturer. After installing a cable, you can prevent fraying of its loose end by press-fitting a cap over it.

Illustration 4–2 shows an English-style brake lever, which uses a cable with a mushroom-shaped fitting. Illustration 4–3 shows a Japanese-style brake lever, which uses a gear cable with a barrel-shaped fitting. Illustration 4–4 shows a typical brake lever found on a 10-speed racing-style bike. These levers take a cable with a mushroom-shaped fitting.

Ways to improvise a cable end when a cable breaks on the road are shown in Illustration 4–5. Even a cable that is too short can be used if its housing is shortened. You can also tie something within an open run of cable to lengthen it sufficiently for use with one of the make-shift end-fittings shown in the illustration.

The loose end of a brake cable is fastened with a pinch bolt on the brake arm as shown in Illustration 4–6. First, be sure the cable is properly seated in the lever and that the adjuster is not tightened all the way down but has been backed off about ⅛ inch. Then use one hand to squeeze the brake pads against the tire rim while pulling the cable taut and finger-tightening the pinch bolt with the other hand. If the cable is not taut enough, try wrapping it around the nose of a pair of pliers and holding it in the desired position while tightening the bolt. Finish tightening the bolt properly after releasing the brake arms. Check the lever operation with full force to make sure you have the right adjustment.

Illustrations 4–7 and 4–8 show two typical gear levers. On the first type, the seat for the cable fitting is open, allowing cables with fittings of different shapes to be used. In this type, the cable is easily replaced and emergency substitution of a brake cable or a knotted end for a closed end is easy. The second

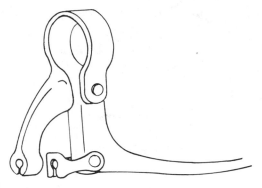

Illustration 4–2. English-style brake lever used on straight-handlebar bikes.

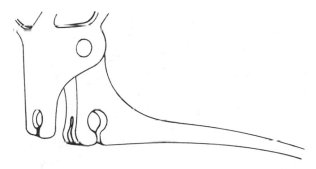

Illustration 4–3. Japanese-style brake lever used on straight-handlebar bikes.

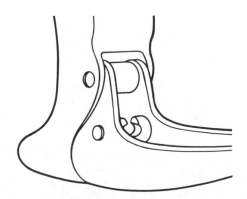

Illustration 4–4. Standard brake lever for 10-speed dropped-handlebar bikes.

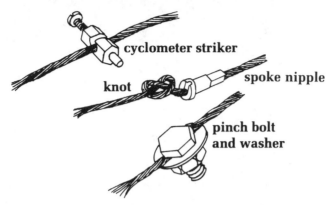

Illustration 4–5. Some on-the-road repairs of broken cable ends.

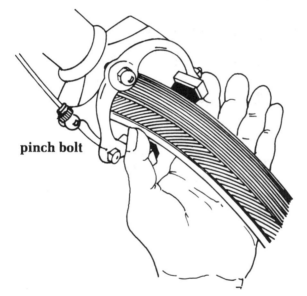

Illustration 4–6. Fastening the loose end of a brake cable.

type of gear lever (Huret and early Simplex) must be dismantled to replace the cable, and the fitting on the cable used must match the seat provided for it. However, in an emergency, a tight knot at the end of any cable will replace the mushroom or barrel end of the original cable. You should frequently inspect the visible portion of the cable where it bends around the lever since a little rust or a broken strand here means a full break is imminent.

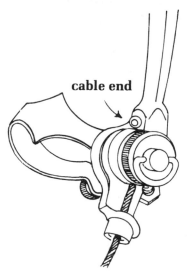

cable end

Illustration 4–7. Gear lever with an open cable seat.

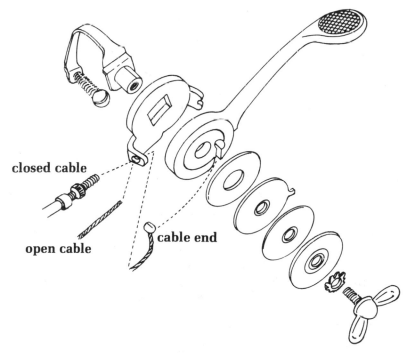

closed cable

open cable

cable end

Illustration 4–8. Gear lever that must be dismantled when replacing cable.

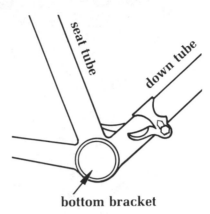

bottom bracket

Illustration 4–9. Bolt-on guides of this type direct open gear cables over the top of the bottom bracket.

Many bicycles have gear cable guides either brazed or bolted to the underside of the bottom bracket. Illustration 4–9 shows a guide for open cables that is bolted to the down tube just before it meets the bottom bracket, allowing the cables to pass over the top of the bottom bracket. Some bicycles use either a fully enclosed cable or a segment of housing for this run. Either one is vulnerable to the inevitable splash from both wheels, and a cable housing is a natural water and grit trap. The open guide has the advantage of being easily cleaned.

Lubrication, as has been pointed out in earlier chapters, is an important part of cable maintenance. The best products to use are those, like WD-40 and LPS-1, that displace water and thus prevent rust. These lubricants also have the advantage of not attracting dirt and grit like ordinary oil and grease. Cables may be the least glamorous components on your bike, but they play vital roles. Keep them clean and well lubricated, and they will return the favor by providing you with many miles of good service.

Credits

The information in this book is drawn from these and other articles from *Bicycling* magazine and from previous bicycling books published by Rodale Press.

"Double-Duty Tools" Andy Di Cyan, "Tool Tips: Tools to Do Double Duty," *Bicycling*, April 1984, pp. 130–35.

"Bicycle Aikido" John S. Allen and Sheldon C. Brown, "Bicycle Aikido: Repair Lessons from the Martial Arts," *Bicycling*, November/December 1983, pp. 16–21.

"A Simple Tool Bag" Eugene LeVee, "A Roll for Your Tools," *Basic Bicycle Repair*, pp. 15–18.

"Bottom Bracket Adjustment" Sheldon C. Brown, "Tool Tips: Bottom Bracket Adjustment," *Bicycling*, June 1983, pp. 142–47.

"Cotter Pin Removal and Installation" Andy Di Cyan, "Cotter Pin Removal and Installation: The Piranha Method," *Bicycling*, June 1984, pp. 168–69; Michael A. Rosen, "How to Overhaul Your Cottered Crank," *Basic Bicycle Repair*, pp. 75–78.

"Removing and Installing Cotterless Cranks" Sheldon C. Brown, "Tool Tips: Cotterless Crank Tools," *Bicycling*, March 1983, pp. 146–57.

"A Crash Course in Rim Repair" Neil Rogers, "Save That Wheel!" *Bicycling*, June 1984, pp. 202–3; John S. Allen, "Emergency Rim Repairs," *Bicycling*, May 1981, pp. 91–93.

"Repairing Tubular Tires" Richard Jow, "The Care and Feeding of Tubular Tires," *Bicycling*, January/February 1983, pp. 133–38.

"Replacing a Broken Spoke" Ray Wolf, "Repairing a Broken Spoke," and Frank Berto, "Why Broken Spokes?" *Basic Bicycle Repair*, pp. 70–75 and p. 75.

"Fitting and Repairing Cables" Chuck Harris, "Fitting and Repairing Cables," *Basic Bicycle Repair*, pp. 85–89.

Photos and Illustrations

Angelo Caggiano: photos 3–6 and 3–7; Mark Lenny: photos 3–2 and 3–3; Gale Minnick: photo 2–3; Photo Dept., Rodale Press: photos 2–2, 2–4, and 2–5; Christie C. Tito: photos 1–1, 1–2, 1–3, 1–4, 2–1, 3–1, 3–8, and 3–9; Sally Shenk Ullman: photos 3–4, 3–5, 4–1, 4–2, 4–3, 4–4, and 4–5. David Bullock: illustrations 1–2, 2–1, 3–1, 4–1, 4–2, 4–3, 4–5, 4–6, 4–7, and 4–8; George Retseck: illustrations 1–1, 4–4, and 4–9; illustration 2–2 adapted from a drawing courtesy of Sutherland Publications.